BATTLES OF THE AMERICAN CIVIL WAR

JONATHAN SUTHERLAND

Airlife

Acknowledgements

The author is indebted to a number of American Civil War enthusiasts and present day photographers, who have generously given permission for their images to be used to illustrate this book. The author wishes to thank them all for their support and hours spent uploading images to enable this book to become a reality.

The American Civil War Society, the largest UK-based American Civil War re-enactment group – www.acws.co.uk. Dave Comeau, a major Canada-based photographer of American Civil War battlefield sites – www.acadiansingray.com/dave_comeau.html. Robert M. and Dr Glen Kleine, grandson and grandfather photographic team from Kentucky – www.aat.eku.edu/Richmond/Battle1.html. The Library of Congress, an outstanding collection of contemporary photographs and illustrations – www.loc.gov. Lisa Mattson, a talented photographer from Pennsylvania with a passion for the Battle of Gettysburg – www.gb1863.com. United States National Archives, the other major US Government archive with a complementary collection of contemporary materials – www.archives.gov. Malcolm Waddy III, a former park ranger at the Fredericksburg battle site and enthusiastic photographer of American Civil War battlefields. He has a staggering number of photographs on his website, which can be viewed at – www.angelfire.com/va2/ageofmalcolm/index.html.

Copyright © 2002 Airlife Publishing Ltd

First published in the UK in 2002
by Airlife Publishing Ltd

Text written by Jonathan Sutherland
Maps drawn by Peter R. Harper

British Library Cataloguing-in-Publication Data
A catalogue record for this book
is available from the British Library

ISBN 1 84037 375 X

All rights reserved. No part of this book may be reproduced or transmitted in any form or by any means, electronic or mechanical including photocopying, recording or by any information storage and retrieval system, without permission from the Publisher in writing.

Typeset by Gray Publishing, Tunbridge Wells, Kent
Printed in Hong Kong

Contact us for a free catalogue that describes the complete range of Airlife books.

Airlife Publishing Ltd
101 Longden Road, Shrewsbury, SY3 9EB, England
E-mail: sales@airlifebooks.com
Website: www.airlifebooks.com

Contents

Introduction

The antagonism between North and South can be traced back to nearly a hundred years before the outbreak of the American Civil War in 1861. Southern nationalism had been growing ever since Washington's time. The South could see that its influence was declining, and it was gradually coming to the opinion that its interests could be served much better outside the Union. The Northern states were far more populous and were wealthier. Southern taxpayers resented Federal policies which, to them, sucked money from the South in order to benefit Northern industry and commerce.

There was also another fundamental difference: the South was a predominantly agricultural economy. A plantation system was in operation which required the widespread use of slaves. The Missouri Compromise of 1850 did not settle the vastly different attitudes towards slavery,

Re-enactment of the Battle of Richmond. (Robert M. Kleine)

and after a decade of disunity the United States slipped into civil war.

The Confederacy emerged with Southern states choosing to secede from the Union. President Abraham Lincoln, having replaced James Buchanan, was determined to meet Southern force with force. Had either he or the Confederate President, Jefferson Davis, realised the carnage that would ensue, it is certain that both would have turned from their course.

In comparison with most European states, the United States had an amateur army. The armed forces had not even been established for a hundred years. West Point classmates would have to quickly choose to whom they pledged their allegiance. The South had always had a military tradition, the North was considered not to produce fighting men of the same calibre. This was to be a conflict that ultimately pitched an emerging industrialised North against a more old-fashioned, agricultural South.

The war was difficult for both North and South, and certainly until the summer of 1863 the Confederacy was winning. The turning points were Gettysburg and Vicksburg. Lee had been turned back and Grant had captured a significant Southern city. Both sides conscripted any able-bodied men they could find. Ultimately the slave question re-emerged, and the North, under Lincoln's guidance, determined that slavery would come to an end and, as significantly, that black troops would be incorporated into the armed forces.

By November 1864 Grant had still failed to penetrate the ring of defences that Lee had set up around Richmond. As the war dragged on it even seemed that Lincoln would lose the presidential election to George B. McClellan.

The Union blockade of the Southern ports was beginning to bite. Gradually the South's opportunities to trade with the rest of the world were being strangled. It did seem for a while that Great Britain or France would fall in beside the Confederacy in their mutual need for one another's business. In the event, deprived of war materials, outpaced by Northern industry and overwhelmed by sheer numbers, the Confederacy began to collapse.

When Union generals finally proved to be the equal of Southern commanders in the field, and when Northern troops showed the verve and determination to carry the fight into the Southern states, the end was inevitable.

During the four years of the war there were over a thousand shooting engagements, from minor skirmishes to major pitched battles. The war raged from the eastern seaboard to the far west, involving thousands whose ancestry and roots can be traced to nearly every corner of the world. Many of the combatants were first-generation Americans, barely established in the country and with little notion of the traditions, causes and meanings of the conflict. Embroiled in the war were both Native Americans and African Americans, who would make their mark on the military history of the United States.

Any collection of battle accounts can only ever hope to reveal a fraction of the American Civil War, but in choosing the engagements my hope is to convey the intensity of the conflict that touched so many parts of the country.

The American Civil War was not the first conflict to be photographed by pioneers of the art, but it is the one war that through the thousands of its images conveys the ruinous waste and carnage in a way that shocked and dismayed the world. For all the martial skills, the uniforms and the glory, not to mention the ideals and beliefs of the North and South, the country is dotted with cemeteries that tell their own mute story of the sacrifices made.

Eastern Theatre

Rich Mountain, Virginia, 11 July 1861
Operations in Western Virginia, June–December 1861

Union:
Major-General George B. McClellan
Brigadier-General William S. Rosecrans
c.2,000 men
(total casualties 46)

Confederate:
Lieutenant-Colonel John Pegram
Brigadier-General Robert S. Garnett
c.1,300 men
(total casualties 300)

In June 1861 McClellan took command of the Union troops in western Virginia, and on 27 June marched south from Clarksburg to face Pegram's troops. Garnett had fortified the two key passes at Laurel Mountain and in the Rich Mountain Pass. Pegram had erected fortifications at Camp Garnett to hold the Rich Mountain Pass which led to Beverly along the Staunton–Parkersburg turnpike. Morris's Union troops marched from Philippi to tackle Garnett at Laurel Hill, and on 11 July Rosecrans led his troops around Pegram's positions to attack him in the rear.

Pegram was caught unprepared as he believed that there was no way Union troops could approach him from behind. But the son of a family which lived at the top of Rich Mountain was pro-Union and showed Rosecrans a dirt road which ran down to the Confederate position. Although they had to struggle through a forest, Rosecrans surprised the 300 Confederate troops holding the rear of the pass at 14.30. Pegram's men managed to hold Rosecrans off for two hours until the pass was overwhelmed. He was then to signal McClellan to launch a frontal attack on Pegram's main positions, but he failed to do this until the following morning. Pegram withdrew during the night to Beverly, and Garnett was forced to abandon Laurel Hill.

Garnett was already being menaced by Morris's brigade, and when he retreated he was pursued and killed at the Battle of Corrick's Ford on 13 July.

As for Pegram's men, they surrendered at Beverly on the same day. Pegram was the first Confederate officer to surrender in the war, but was later exchanged and fought with distinction at the Battle of Stone's River.

The victory at Rich Mountain propelled McClellan to assume command of the Army of the Potomac, and by October 1862 Rosecrans was in command of the Army of Cumberland, facing Pegram once more at Stone's River.

First Manassas (First Bull Run), Virginia, 21 July 1861
The Manassas Campaign, July 1861

Union:
Brigadier-General Irvin McDowell
c.35,000 men (18,572 engaged)
(total casualties *c*.2,896–2,950)

Confederate:
Brigadier-General Joseph E. Johnston
Army of the Shenandoah
Brigadier-General P.G.T. Beauregard
Army of the Potomac
c.32,500 men (18,053 engaged)
(total casualties *c*.1,750–1,982)

First Manassas, or Bull Run, was the first major land battle for the armies based in Virginia. Effectively both of the armies were untried, but it was clear that Washington was expecting a crushing victory by its army, led by McDowell, who had impeccable credentials.

McDowell planned to overwhelm Beauregard at Manassas whilst Patterson held Johnston's troops in the valley. McDowell launched his offensive on 16 July, taking $2\frac{1}{2}$ days to march the twenty miles to Centreville. The vanguard of McDowell's army was led by Tyler, who ran into Confederates at Blackburn's Ford on the Bull Run, where a skirmish turned into a Union rout. McDowell realised that a frontal attack would be suicidal with his 'green' troops. He therefore used 19 and 20 July to scout the Bull Run crossings in order to find a route that he could march along with a view to facing Beauregard in the open rather than behind his earthworks.

Lead elements of Johnston's troops left Winchester on the 18th and marched to Paris and then on to Piedmont. They then boarded trains which brought them to the Manassas Junction at 13.00 on the 19th.

Finally, on the 20th, McDowell had thrashed out his strategy and he determined that his main assault would be made the following day. Union troops

Stone Bridge looking west at the battle of First Bull Run. *(Malcolm Waddy III)*

began leaving in the early hours of the morning, and by 05.30 Tyler's men were near Stone Bridge. It was held by 1,000 Confederates. Two hours passed without the Union troops trying to push the crossing, but eventually the Confederates pulled back and established a new position on Matthew's Hill, after they had seen the weight of the Union column which was now crossing Sudley Springs.

At 10.00 Burnside's Union troops led the assault, which rolled over the hill, forcing the Confederates to fall back to Matthew's House. More Confederates were being fed in to their left, but not enough to stem the Union tide. The Union troops advanced past Stone House and towards Henry Hill. The morning phase of the battle had been won.

The Confederate line now stretched from the Manassas–Sudley road up to Henry House, then to

Robinson House, where it dipped south of Young's Branch. McDowell resumed his attacks at 13.00, with four brigades aiming to capture Henry Hill. The Confederates were swept aside, losing both Henry House and Robinson House. From here they encountered Jackson's Confederates, who held and blasted them with musketry and artillery fire. It was at this battle that he earned the nickname of 'Stonewall' Jackson.

Foolishly McDowell now moved his hitherto very effective artillery batteries near Henry House. At 15.00 one of Jackson's regiments marched out of the grove of trees that they were holding and in a devastating volley killed 54 gunners and 104 horses. As the Confederates swarmed over the battery, Stuart's Confederate cavalry swept out and routed Union infantry that had been behind the guns. McDowell was not finished; he counter-attacked, and the guns

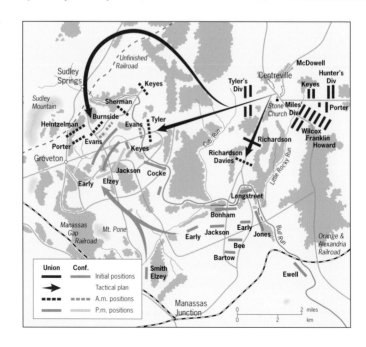

changed hands on three occasions. Finally the guns remained in Confederate hands.

The tide turned eventually at 16.00, when the Union army began to disintegrate. Almost as one they decided that they had taken enough. The Confederates were eager to finish the matter once and for all, and Johnston directed Early and Kirby Smith to advance on the exposed flank of Howard's brigade, which was still trying to push the Confederates off Henry Hill. Howard's men ran and took with them what was left of any semblance of order in the Union army. As the fugi-tives fled back across Bull Run, a lucky Confederate shot destroyed a wagon in the centre span of Cub Run Bridge. Any hope of an orderly Union retreat evaporated as soldiers and hundreds of civilians, who had hired buggies in Washington to witness the Confederates being thoroughly beaten, ran for their lives. The Confederates were too disorganised themselves to pursue, and contented themselves with collecting prisoners. McDowell's army had been decisively defeated but was reorganised in Washington, and on 26 July a new commander, George B. McClellan, was installed.

Ball's Bluff, Virginia, 21 October 1861
Operations on the Upper Potomac, 1861

Both sides had around 1,700 men engaged. Union losses were 200 killed and wounded, with 700 captured. Confederate losses were minimal.

After the first battle of Manassas, the 7th Brigade of the Confederate Army of Potomac was sent to occupy Leesburg, which lay on the left flank of the Confederate lines.

On 15 October, General Banks's division of the Union army was fifteen miles east of Leesburg, supported by Stone's Division at Poolesville, eight miles north of Leesburg. Their purpose, similar to that of Evans's Seventh Brigade, was to protect the flank of the Union army.

By 19 October, McCall's Union Division had advanced to Dranesville, fifteen miles from Leesburg, supported by Smith's Division advancing on a parallel road. Evans, meanwhile, entrenched his men along Goose Creek, three miles south-east of Leesburg. McClellan, the Union commander, realised that this might offer an opportunity to capture Leesburg and outmanoeuvre the Confederates. Accordingly, he told Stone to make a show of attempting to cross the Potomac River at Leesburg so that the Confederates would move back and more ground could be taken.

At 06.00 on 21 October, Evans discovered that Stone's Division had actually crossed the Potomac at Edward's Ferry and at Ball's Bluff. Elements of Baker's Brigade from Stone's Division had crossed at midnight and at dawn were approaching Leesburg. Evans directed Colonels Hunton and Jenifer to form a line at Leesburg and throw the enemy back into the river. By noon, both forces were in place, the Union troops having had to contend with a difficult crossing of the river on three small boats that could only carry 25 men at a time.

The Confederates immediately advanced, fearing that the longer they waited the more Union reinforcements would move up. By 14.00 Stone was ferrying more men across the Edward's Ferry. Half an hour later Evans moved batteries to check Stone's new move and called up Colonel Burt's 18th Mississippi to attack the Union left, and at 15.00 reinforce Burt with Featherston's 17th. The move was working, and by 18.00 Burt and Featherston had forced the Union troops back to the river. With one last attack, a bayonet charge, the Confederates broke through to the river bank; all around Union troops were surrendering.

The death of Col. Edward D. Baker at Ball's Bluff. (Library of Congress)

3

Shenandoah, Virginia, 23 March to 10 June 1862

Shenandoah Valley Campaign 1862

Kernstown 23 March 1862
Union:
Brigadier-General James Shields
c.7,000 men
(total casualties 590)

Confederate:
Major-General Thomas J. Jackson
c.2,742 engaged
(total casualties 718)

McDowell 8 May 1862
Union:
Brigadier-General Robert Schenck
c.2,268 men
(total casualties 256)

Confederate:
Major-General Thomas J. Jackson
c.6,000 men
(total casualties 499)

Harper's Ferry 20–26 May 1862
Union:
Brigadier-General Rufus Saxton
c.7,000 men
(total casualties 15)

Confederate:
Major-General Thomas J. Jackson*

Front Royal, Middletown, Newtown and Winchester 23–25 May 1862
Union:
Major-General Nathaniel P. Banks
c.9,178 men
(total casualties 2,019–3,050)

Confederate:
Major-General Thomas J. Jackson*

Cross Keys, Mount Carmel, Strasburg, Woodstock, Mount Jackson and Harrisonburg 1–9 June 1862
Union:
Major-General John Frémont
c.10,500 men
(total casualties *c*.786)

Confederate:
Major-General Thomas J. Jackson*

Port Republic 8–9 June 1862
Brigadier-General James Shields
c.9,000 men
(total casualties 4,609)

Confederate:
Major-General Thomas J. Jackson
20 May to 10 June
c.13,000–17,000 men
(total casualties for campaign 1,878)*

Shortly after the First Battle of Manassas (Bull Run), Stonewall Jackson was promoted to Major-General and was assigned the valley district as his military command, with a force on paper of around 10,000 men.

The winter in the valley was not kind to the Confederates, and by the beginning of March Jackson had around 5,000 effectives. There had been a considerable number of Union troops in and around the valley, but McClellan was gathering as many men as he could east of the mountains. This left General Shields at Winchester with an army of between 8,000 and 10,000 men. Jackson was determined to make

4　*General Shields at the Battle of Winchester. (Library of Congress)*

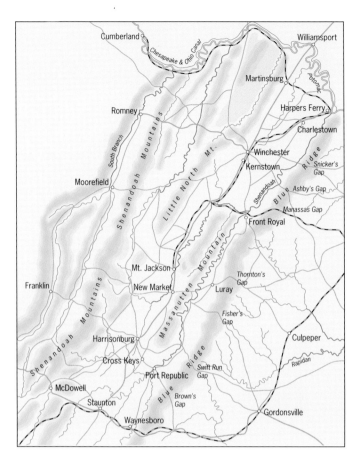

McClellan rethink and commit more troops to the valley, taking the pressure off Lee.

On 23 March Jackson occupied the ridge at Kernstown, just four miles from Winchester. Conveniently Shields attacked him. Jackson was forced to retreat, but Shields did not take the opportunity to pursue. Jackson fell back on Swift Run Gap and was reinforced on 1 May, giving him a command of between 13,000 and 15,000 men.

Union troops were now commanded by Frémont, with 4,000 at McDowell, 2,500 near Franklin, a further 20,000 moving towards Franklin and another 20,000 near Harrisonburg. There were further reserves, which took the whole Union force to around 80,000, of whom 65,000 were in the valley.

By early May Jackson was at Port Republic, but his cavalry were keeping a close eye on the Union troops. Jackson marched from Charlottesville and boarded trains at Mechum's River Station, then headed west and into Staunton. By 8 May he was three miles east of McDowell; he fought a battle here which routed Schenck's and Milroy's men, who fled towards Franklin, pursued by Jackson's cavalry. Jackson himself fell back to Staunton. He then marched to Harrisonburg and by forced marches reached New Market in two days. Here he found Banks had dug in near Strasburg, but had a large detachment at Front Royal, eight miles away. Jackson fell on him and drove Banks through Winchester and across the Potomac. Jackson then disappeared again, having struck at Front Royal on 23 May.

By 25 May Frémont had set out with 14,000 men from Franklin to try to cut off Jackson. Jackson was heading for Harrisonburg and Shields was marching to aid Frémont. Jackson turned at Cross Keys on 8 June and decisively defeated Frémont there. After the battle, leaving Ewell to cover his retreat, Jackson marched back to Port Republic with a view to attacking Shield's command the next morning.

On 9 June Jackson was ready to move at daybreak, having found Shields's army in the vicinity of the Lewis Farm, just below the town of Port Republic. The battle was a close-run thing, and luckily for Jackson he had taken the precaution of destroying the bridges across the Shenandoah River, so when Frémont arrived on the battlefield to aid Shields, he could only watch in agony as Jackson beat his fellow general.

Jackson now pulled back to Swift Run Gap to rest his men. A few days later Jackson's army was on the right flank of McClellan on the Chickahominy River.

From the date of Jackson's arrival in Staunton to the final battle at Port Republic, his troops marched 40 miles from Staunton to McDowell, 110 to Front Royal, 20 more to Winchester, and 75 to Port Republic, covering nearly 250 miles and fighting four battles, all of which were Confederate victories.

Williamsburg (Fort Magruder), Virginia, 5 May 1862

Peninsular Campaign, March–September 1862

Union:
Major-General George B. McClellan
c.40,768 men
(total casualties 2,283)

Confederate:
Major-General James Longstreet
c.31,823 men
(total casualties 1,560)

Williamsburg was the first major battle of the Peninsular Campaign. The Confederates had retreated to the Warwick Yorktown area and built a series of fortifications. Fort Magruder commanded the roads leading up the peninsula to Williamsburg.

On 3 May the Confederates had been beaten at Yorktown, and McClellan had sent cavalry, supported by Hooker's Division, to chase the Confederates away. By noon on 4 May it was clear that the Confederates had dug in around Fort Magruder. Hooker's men did not arrive until shortly after daybreak on the 5th; he had the assurance of more troops arriving within two hours, and the bulk of McClellan's army just four hours away.

The initial attacks forced the Confederates back into the fort, but the promised reinforcements failed to arrive. Longstreet, taking advantage of the situa-

tion, strengthened his line and launched three counter-attacks, which were all beaten off with heavy losses.

Throughout the afternoon until 17.00, possession of the outer defences changed several times. Finally, Brigadier-General Kearny's Division arrived and stabilised Hooker's hold on the perimeter.

Meanwhile, Hancock's Brigade appeared on the Confederate left and occupied two uncontested redoubts on Cub Creek; from here he was able to shell the Confederate flank and rear. Hancock also managed to fend off a badly organised and misconceived counter-attack hastily organised by Longstreet. He sent in Hill and Early; the latter was wounded, and the former later described the attack as 'one of the most awful things I ever saw'. Again the Union army failed to reinforce at the crucial time, and instead Hancock was ordered to pull back.

During the night the Confederates withdrew towards Richmond, and McClellan was happy to claim a victory. In actual fact the battle was inconclusive, but the Confederates had delayed the Union offensive on the peninsula.

Had it not been for Lee's foresight in preparing the defences then it is doubtful whether the Confederates could have held McClellan, and it is probable that the Union army would have overrun the Confederate rearguard.

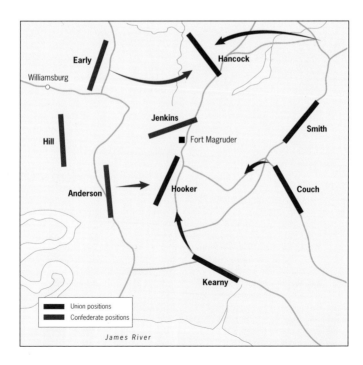

Front Royal (Guard Hill, Cedarville), Virginia, 23 May 1862

Jackson's Shenandoah Valley Campaign, 1862

Union:
Colonel John R. Kenly
c.1,063 men
(total casualties 904)

Confederate:
Major-General Thomas J. Jackson
c.3,000 men
(total casualties 56)

Shortly after the First Battle of Manassas, Stonewall Jackson was promoted to Major-General and took command of Confederate troops in the Shenandoah Valley in November 1861. By May 1862 his Little Army was ready to launch a major offensive. Front Royal is a prime example of how his supreme tactical genius ran rings around the more cumbersome Union troops operating in the valley. Jackson was able to march his troops at least thirty miles in twenty-four hours, which resulted in his infantry being given the title of 'Jackson's Foot Cavalry'.

The Union commander in the valley, Major-General Nathaniel P. Banks, who faced him in the latter days of May 1862, seemed completely unaware of where Jackson would strike next. Banks believed that Jackson was at New Market and had fortified Strasburg and left a large detachment at Front Royal, about eight miles from the main Union positions.

Jackson crossed the Massanutten Mountain and arrived at Front Royal in the early afternoon of 23 May. His attack was spearheaded by the Louisiana Tigers and the First Maryland. Jackson achieved complete surprise and overwhelmed the pickets around the thousand-strong Union garrison. The Confederate attack pushed Kenly's men onto Camp Hill, where they resisted for a while, but they were then pushed onto Guard Hill. Kenly was completely outmanoeuvred and retreated towards Cedarville. Jackson sent his cavalry under Colonel Flournoy and blocked their retreat, forcing the remaining 900 Union soldiers to surrender. As a result, Banks was forced to abandon Strasburg and retreat on Winchester.

Jackson continued his advance and caught Banks at Newtown the following day, capturing most of Banks's supplies and many more prisoners. After encountering Ewell on 25 May, Banks slipped across the Potomac; he had lost over 3,000 men since the middle of May.

According to Kenly, Jackson attacked at 14.00 and managed to maintain cohesion until 17.00. It was only after this that his men were overwhelmed, particularly after the two cavalry charges led by Flournoy.

Fair Oaks (Seven Pines), Virginia, 31 May to 1 June 1862

Peninsular Campaign, March–September 1862

Union:
Major-General George B. McClellan
Army of the Potomac
c.98,008 men (51,543 engaged)
(total casualties 5,031)

Confederate:
General Joseph E. Johnston
c.53,688–73,928 men (39,000 engaged)
(total casualties 6,134)

The end of May 1862 found McClellan's Army of the Potomac just twelve miles from Richmond. He had positioned two of his corps south of the Chickahominy River and three to the north. McDowell's Corps was moving up from Fredericksburg and planned to reinforce McClellan.

Unfortunately, because of the heavy rains, the river was unusually swollen, which gave the Confederates a chance to smash the Union III Corps (Heintzelman) and IV Corps (Keyes) stationed south of the river. It was a complex plan that relied on pinpoint timing and navigation. Four Confederate columns would converge on Heintzelman and Keyes using three different roads.

Johnston thrashed out the plans, giving verbal instructions to the Confederate commanders. As soon as the manoeuvres began, there were problems. Longstreet's men marched up the wrong road, which had been assigned to D.H. Hill's and Benjamin Huger's columns. Consequently, it was not until 13.00 on 31 May that Hill's men were in position to open the attack against the enemy. Even then Hill was unsupported, but his troops pushed back Keyes's men. Finally, Longstreet arrived and managed to throw in enough men to force the Union line further back.

Whiting's charge at Fair Oaks itself went in at 16.00, but Sumner's II Corps had managed to obtain reinforcements and the Confederate attack was held.

The Battle of Fair Oaks. *(Library of Congress)*

As fighting petered out at 18.00, Johnston was seriously wounded and replaced by Major-General Gustavus W. Smith. In the morning the Confederates attacked again, but by now the Union army was prepared and held them off on all fronts. Smith's failure to make any headway led to his replacement on the orders of Jefferson Davis. His replacement was none other than Robert E. Lee. The purpose and opportu-nity as far as the Confederates were concerned had passed, and Lee ordered a withdrawal from the area.

It was a tactical victory for the Union, despite the fact that McClellan had nearly lost two of his corps. Had it not been for the confusion and delays on the roads to Fair Oaks, McClellan's troops would have been destroyed. Lee and McClellan would meet again very soon.

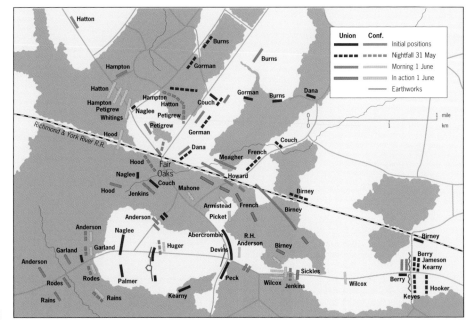

Union:
Major-General George B. McClellan
Army of the Potomac
150 infantry regiments
10 cavalry regiments
136 artillery pieces
c.115,000 men
(total casualties *c*.15,849)

Confederate:
General Robert E. Lee
Army of Northern Virginia
173 infantry regiments
12 cavalry regiments
71 batteries of artillery
c.81,000 men
(total casualties *c*.19,749–20,135)

On 2 April 1862 McClellan had assembled the largest army ever seen on the North American continent at Fort Monroe at the tip of the peninsula between the York and James Rivers. His troops were just sixty miles from Richmond. From the beginning there were difficulties: the maps were incorrect and the roads wrongly marked, crossing points were few across the numerous creeks and rivers. But, unperturbed, McClellan decided to press on. Rather than march towards Richmond he chose to besiege Yorktown, which at the time was the strongest point in the Confederate defence line.

No sooner had McClellan completed his preparations for his attack than the Confederate General Johnston abandoned the town. An indecisive rearguard action was fought at Williamsburg on 5 May as the Confederates retreated towards Richmond. Significantly the Confederate abandonment of Yorktown opened up the York River to the Union fleet, and a resupply base was established at

White House Landing on the Pamunkey River just twenty miles east of Richmond.

As Union troops advanced, the Confederates were forced to abandon Norfolk on 10 May and wreck their own ironclad, *the Virginia*. This opened up the James River as far as Drewry's Bluff, only nine miles south of Richmond. A naval engagement here on 15 May was repulsed by Confederate batteries.

McClellan's army was camped astride the Chickahominy River with his III and IV Corps on the south and his II, V and VI Corps on the north. McDowell's Corps marched south from Fredericksburg to join McClellan's troops on the north of the Chickahominy. All now seemed set for McClellan to move against Johnston.

Crucially, whilst these developments took place on the peninsula, Stonewall Jackson was rampaging through the Shenandoah Valley. This caused the recall of McDowell's Corps to the north in order to protect Washington.

During May heavy rain added to McClellan's difficulties by making it increasingly difficult to co-ordinate his split command. On 31 May Johnston moved against the two Union corps on the south of the river, and at the Battle of Fair Oaks (Seven Pines), from 31 May to 1 June 1862, the Union troops managed to hold their ground with the assistance of elements of II Corps, which had succeeded in crossing the river to support them. It was a poorly executed assault by the Confederates and this was compounded by the fact that Johnston was severely wounded. This meant that his command of the Army of Northern Virginia passed to Robert E. Lee on 1 June. Under his command the Confederate forces withdrew towards Richmond, but later launched a counter-offensive known as the Seven Days Battles. Lee's offensive pushed McClellan back down the

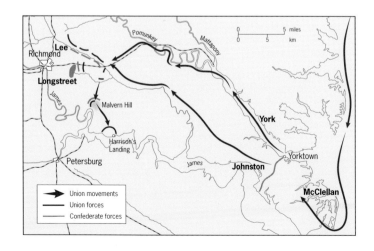

9

peninsula until he had reached Harrison's Landing, which effectively brought the Peninsular Campaign to an end.

Throughout the campaign, despite the impending danger to their capital, the Confederates were in high spirits, as is amply described by the following exchange between Johnston and Hood just after the Battle of Williamsburg:

'Tell him', Johnston said, 'that a force of the enemy estimated at from 3–5,000, have landed on York River, and they are ravaging the country. His brigade must immediately check the advance of this force. He is to feel the enemy gently and fall back, avoiding an engagement and drawing them from under the protection of their gunboats, as an ample force will be sent

in their rear, and if he can draw them a few miles from the river, their capture is certain.'

In the event, Hood's Texans drove the Union troops back to their gunboats and killed and captured several hundred. After the engagement Johnston said: 'General Hood, have you given an illustration of the Texas idea of feeling an enemy gently and falling back? What would your Texans have done, Sir, if I ordered them to charge and drive back the enemy?' Hood replied 'I suppose, General, they would have driven them into the river, and tried to swim out and capture the gunboats.' Johnston's response was: 'Teach your Texans that the first duty of a soldier is literally to obey orders.'

Yorktown, Virginia, 5 April to 4 May 1862
Peninsular Campaign, 1862

Union:
Major-General George B. McClellan
Army of the Potomac
c.100,000 men

Confederate:
General John B. Magruder
Army of the Peninsula
c.9,300 men (2,500 in garrison)

(total casualties 320)

McClellan's vast Army of the Potomac marched out of Fort Monroe and encountered Magruder's tiny Army of the Peninsula at Yorktown on the Warwick River.

Magruder allowed McClellan to believe that Yorktown was held by a strong Confederate contingent. This persuaded the Union commander that he would have to stand and pinch out this Confederate position before he could continue his march on Richmond. Consequently, he brought up heavy siege artillery and prepared fortifications all around Yorktown. Meanwhile, General Johnston reinforced Magruder and bolstered his garrison.

The most significant action of this phase of the Peninsular Campaign was the engagement at Dam No. 1, or Lee's Mill, on 16 April. McClellan had sent troops to probe the Confederate line in search of a weakness that he could exploit. Union troops suc-

ceeded in pushing the Confederates back, but McClellan failed to exploit this temporary advantage and waited for two more weeks before Union gunboats moved up the York River to West Point to outflank the Warwick line.

As McClellan planned the last stages of his intended offensive, which would open on 4 May, the Confederate garrison slipped out of Yorktown and headed towards Williamsburg.

The delays caused to McClellan by the Confederates stubbornly holding onto Yorktown allowed the Confederates to destroy the fortifications of Norfolk, and wreck the shipyards there so that they did not fall into enemy hands. It is difficult to understand why McClellan, with his vast superiority in numbers, failed to launch a determined assault on Yorktown. As General Magruder himself later stated in his official report, the Confederates were astonished as well:

'To my surprise he [McClellan] permitted day after day to pass without an assault. In every direction in front of our lines, through the intervening woods, and along the open fields, earthworks began to appear. Through the energetic action of the Government, reinforcements began to pour in, and each hour the Army of the Peninsula grew stronger and stronger, until anxiety passed from my mind as to the result of an attack upon us.'

10

Port Republic, Virginia, 9 June 1862
Jackson's Shenandoah Valley Campaign, 1862

Union:
Brigadier-General Erastus Tyler
c.3,500 men
(total casualties 1,002)

Confederate:
Major-General Thomas J. Jackson
c.6,000 men
(total casualties 816)

The two battles of Port Republic and Cross Keys were amongst the most decisive in Stonewall Jackson's 1862 Shenandoah Valley Campaign.

On 8 June Jackson had defeated Major-General Frémont, who had been approaching from Harrisonburg, at the Battle of Cross Keys. Meanwhile, Jackson had sent part of a division to hold Brigadier-General Shields's Union troops who were advancing towards Port Republic. Having defeated Frémont, Jackson's troops marched through the night of 8/9 June to attack Shields's brigades, who were being commanded by Tyler.

The Confederates attacked Tyler's positions, which were at right angles to the Shenandoah River. Initially assaults nearest the river failed to shift the Union line, but a flanking move around the Union left flank forced a series of Union counter-attacks which failed to secure their position. Tyler was forced to retreat and, as Confederate troops watching Frémont joined Jackson at Port Republic, they burned the North River Bridge behind them. This meant that Frémont arrived on the battlefield too late to help Tyler; he could only watch from the other side of the river, helplessly, as Tyler was defeated.

These two actions, having crippled the Union troops, allowed Jackson to march his troops through the Upper and Middle Shenandoah Valley to reinforce General Robert E. Lee against McClellan's army which was threatening Richmond.

Jackson's attention to detail shows his remarkable understanding of the terrain:

'Winder will cross the river at daybreak and attack Shields on the Lewis Farm. Taylor will move through the woods on the side of the mountain … and rush upon their left flank. By 10 o'clock we shall get them on the run. Three miles below Lewis's there is a defile on the Luray Road. Shields may rally and make a stand there. If he does, I can't reach him with the field batteries on account of the woods. You can carry your 12-pounder howitzers on the mules up the mountainside, and at some good place unpack and shell the enemy out of the defile, and the cavalry will do the rest.'

Union artillery. (American Civil War Society)

Union:
Major-General George B. McClellan
Army of the Potomac
150 infantry regiments
10 cavalry regiments
136 artillery pieces
c.115,000 men
(total casualties *c*.15,849)

Confederate:
General Robert E. Lee
Army of Northern Virginia
173 infantry regiments
12 cavalry regiments
71 batteries of artillery
c.81,000 men
(total casualties *c*.19,749–20,135)

McClellan, in command of the Union forces on the peninsula, had been under constant pressure from Abraham Lincoln during the first two weeks of June to move on the Confederates. As it was, he ordered his corps commanders to move on 25 June.

As McClellan's troops advanced along the Williamsburg Road with the intention of deploying guns to bombard Richmond, they were attacked at Oak Grove (French's Field, King's School House). The swampy ground made deployment difficult, and the battle ended inconclusively when darkness fell. McClellan had run into a major Confederate offensive. Casualties were even, with just over 500 losses on each side.

The second inevitable battle occurred the following day at Beaver Dam Creek (Mechanicsville, Ellerson's Mill), when Lee hit McClellan's right flank north of the Chickahominy River. Confederate Generals A.P. Hill and D.H. Hill launched a series of assaults against Porter's Union V Corps, which was entrenched in good positions behind Beaver Dam

Creek. The Confederates suffered enormous losses. Lee had hoped that Jackson, marching from the Shenandoah, would arrive in time to have an impact on the battle. He was wrong, and Jackson arrived too late, but his appearance did force Porter to withdraw to Boatswain's Creek near Gaines's Mill. Although the sides in this battle were equal in match, the Confederates suffered three times as many casualties as the Union troops.

On the following day, reunited with Jackson, Lee launched another assault against Porter's V Corps, which was in strong defensive positions at Boatswain's Swamp. Porter managed to hold on until the late afternoon, but at dusk a final Confederate assault drove him back towards the river. This battle was the turning point in the Seven Days, and McClellan's march on Richmond had been stopped. Casualties were extremely high, with over 15,500 dead, the Confederates having suffered more severely.

The fourth battle at Savage's Station occurred on 29 June whilst McClellan's army was withdrawing towards the James River. The Union rearguard was hit by Confederates, but the engagement was inconclusive as Lee could not support the assault in time. Some 2,500 wounded Union troops were captured when a field hospital was overrun.

At White Oak Swamp, Union commander Franklin opposed Stonewall Jackson's divisions as they tried to cross the White Oak Bridge. This was an intense artillery duel, with around 500 casualties. Whilst this battle was raging, the main conflict was occurring two miles further south at Frayser's Farm, or Glendale. Three Confederate divisions had caught up with the retreating Union army, and at Willis Church they had routed McCall's Division, capturing the commander. Union commanders Hooker and Kearny counter-attacked and secured the line of retreat along the Willis Church Road. Stonewall Jackson was still delayed at White Oak Swamp, and a Confederate attempt to turn the Union left at Turkey

12 *Guns situated on Malvern Hill during the battles of the Seven Days. (Malcolm Waddy III)*

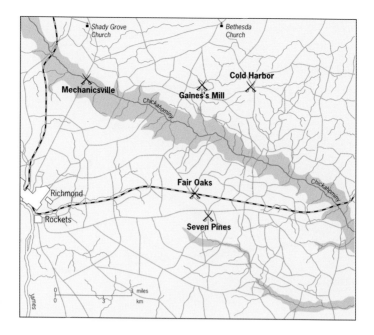

Bridge was beaten off by Union gunboats on the James River. This had been Lee's best opportunity to cut off McClellan before he crossed the James River.

The final battle of the Seven Days took place at Malvern Hill (Poindexter's Farm), where McClellan had established a formidable defensive position around the hill. Lee launched wave after wave of uncoordinated assaults, which resulted in over 5,300 casualties for no gain. McClellan, having beaten off Lee, withdrew to Harrison's Landing, where he could be sure of artillery support from the Union gunboats.

This was the end of the Seven Days Battles and the Peninsular Campaign. McClellan's army was no longer a threat to Richmond. Secure in this knowledge, Lee was able to send Jackson along the Rapidan River to tackle Major-General John Pope's troops and begin the Northern Virginia Campaign.

General Longstreet expertly summed up the characteristics of the two major Confederate commanders at the time:

'Lee's orders were always well considered and well chosen. He depended almost too much on his officers for their execution. Jackson was a very skilful man ... but when pitted against the best of the Federal commanders he did not appear so well.'

Gaines's Mill, Virginia, 27–28 June 1862
Peninsular Campaign, 1862

Union:
Major-General George B. McClellan
Army of the Potomac
59 infantry regiments
*c.*4 cavalry regiments
124 artillery pieces
*c.*35,000
(total casualties 6,837)

Confederate:
General Robert E. Lee
Army of Northern Virginia
125 infantry regiments
76 artillery pieces
*c.*56,000
(total casualties 8,300)

Gaines's Mill was the penultimate battle of the Peninsular Campaign and the last in the series of battles known as the Seven Days. Following the Battle of Mechanicsville on 26 June and the arrival of Confederate commander Stonewall Jackson, Union General McClellan withdrew to the east of Gaines's Mill.

The new Union position was spread along a natural defence in the shape of Boatswain's Swamp. The Confederates advanced on the morning of the 27th, initially meeting light resistance. They were gradually overtaking Union stragglers, but by 14.00 Lee realised that McClellan had turned to fight him.

The first Confederate attack swept through Gaines's Mill and across the Cold Harbor Road, straight towards the slope of Boatswain's Swamp. Here they formed a firing line to oppose the Union troops. 13

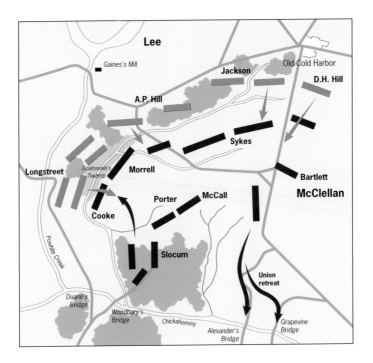

Meanwhile, Lee had arrived and organised an attack along the three-quarter of a mile front; it was a disaster, and by 16.00 fresh Union troops were arriving, but so, too, had Jackson. Lee ordered Longstreet to attack the far left of the Union line to suck in Union reserves whilst his main assault would be on the extreme right, led by Jackson and D.H. Hill. By 17.30 the Union line on the right was giving way, and by 19.00 the Union troops were so hard-pressed that they were withdrawing along the whole front.

Jackson continued to press on the right and gave his men the orders: 'Tell them this affair must hang in suspense no longer. Sweep the field with the bayonet.'

Still fresh Union troops were crossing the Chickahominy River but had not yet reached the battle line. To hold the Union defences troops had to be pulled out of the centre. Men were desperately needed to hold Longstreet and support the Union troops facing Jackson and D.H. Hill.

The Confederates were still pushing forward, and the Union left was the first to go. In the centre and on the right the Union troops were falling back in good order. The Union had set up a fourteen-gun battery to the rear, and it was hoped that the troops could reform behind the guns.

Suddenly Cooke's V US Cavalry and other elements of mounted units fell into line beside the artillery pieces and then charged the advancing Confederates. The Confederates unleashed a shattering volley, and the cavalry retreated straight through the battery, closely followed by screaming Confederates. The last hope for the Union army to hold a line had passed, but with the help of

elements of the Union II Corps, a retreat was achieved. McClellan's men fell back across the Chickahominy River; the last to leave was Cooke's command.

With the exception of A.P. Hill's Division that had taken the brunt of the fighting from the first shots, the Confederate army was still in a sound fighting condition. They had lost around 8,000 killed and wounded and had captured over 3,000 Union troops.

It is said that the turning point of the battle occurred when Hood's IV Texas approached to within ten yards of the Union defence line. Here they opened fire at close range and caused enormous panic. Hood led his men in pursuit of the retreating Union soldiers, followed by Georgians and South Carolinians.

McClellan's troops had fought well but they had been outmanoeuvred. More grievous was the loss of all of the supplies, which, it is said, took quartermasters back in Richmond three days to sort out. The Union initiative had been lost and with it McClellan's reputation. He had persuaded Abraham Lincoln that they should not face the Confederates at Manassas, ten miles from Washington, but should use their superior manoeuvrability to land on the peninsula and threaten Richmond itself.

This was not the end of the Peninsular Campaign. McClellan and Lee would meet once more at Malvern Hill on 1 July, when Confederate infantry would be shredded by massed Union artillery.

Despite all of McClellan's abilities, perhaps the Confederate General Johnston summed him up in the best way by saying: 'Nobody but McClellan would have hesitated to attack.'

Union:
Major-General Nathaniel Banks
Army of Virginia
II Corps
Augur's Division
Williams's Division
c.8,030 men
(total casualties 1,400)

Confederate:
Major-General Thomas J. Jackson
Army of Northern Virginia
Jackson's Corps
c.16,868 men
(total casualties 1,307)

On 26 June, General John Pope was given command of the newly formed Army of Virginia. Pope's Union army drove south along the Orange and Alexandria Railroad, with Crawford and Banks's Divisions nearing Culpepper.

The Confederates, responding to Pope's move, sent Major-General Jackson with his troops to Gordonsville in July. Pope clearly meant to take the railroad junction at Gordonsville, and consequently headed south into Culpepper County.

The two armies met south of Culpepper on a hill called Cedar Mountain and along the stream nearby, called Cedar Run. Jackson knew that Banks's men were the vanguard of the main Union army and determined to defeat him before he could be reinforced.

Banks's men, about 8,000 strong, were in the Cedar Mountain vicinity by noon. They halted, awaiting the arrival of Ricketts's Division, which was coming up in support.

Jackson had deployed along the northern edge of the mountain with Trimble, Forno and Early (of Ewell's Division) on the right, and Taliaferro and Garnett on the left. The line was supported by A.P. Hill's Division. Facing them were Augur's men on the Union left and Williams's on the right.

Early and Taliaferro advanced continuously at 15.00. Banks's men were formed-up on the opposite side of the valley on the north-east of Cedar Run. Augur pushed Geary and Prince forward, meeting the Confederates on a cultivated plateau just south of the Culpepper–Gordonsville Road.

Hidden in cover on the Union right was Bayard's cavalry, consisting of four regiments of Union

The Battle of Cedar Mountain. (Library of Congress)

cavalry. Banks threw in Crawford's infantry onto the left of the Confederate troops opposing Augur's Division. For a time the advantage lay with Banks, but Jackson sent in fresh brigades, those of Hill's Division, to counter Prince and Geary. By now it was 18.00, and the fighting reached its height when Banks sent in his last fresh infantry, Greene's brigade of Augur's Division and Gordon's brigade of Williams's Division. Banks's artillery was losing the duel with the Confederate guns on the mountainsides; he knew that his troops would be pounded if he did not attempt to settle the battle now.

In response to the Union reinforcements Ewell threw in his brigades from the right, and Thomas's brigade was brought up to close the gap between Early and Forno. With increasing opposition in the shape of superior numbers, Banks's men began to give ground. Rather belatedly, Banks unleashed Bayard's cavalry just as Branch's Confederates were being brought up in support. The Union cavalry were repulsed, and with that the Union troops began to retire.

Banks's men, still in good order, retreated back across Cedar Run, and under the cover of darkness were reinforced by Ricketts. General Pope had accompanied him to see the situation for himself.

The next day, 10 August, was a Sunday, and under a flag of truce, the Union army collected their wounded and buried their dead. For some time it appeared that the battle would resume, but under cover of night Jackson withdrew his troops back across the Rapidan and Robinson Rivers. Pope chose not to pursue. The time would come when Pope would face Jackson. He only had nineteen days to wait before the Confederate master-strategist defeated him at Second Manassas.

The battle is particularly significant for a number of reasons. Cedar Mountain was the only battle in which Jackson drew his sword. When Banks's men had gained the upper hand early on in the battle and his men were falling back, it is said that he personally led the counter-attack. His prompt and courageous action turned what could so easily have been a Confederate rout into a victory. As General Branch wrote on 13 August:

'The enemy's cavalry attempted to charge us in 2 columns, but the fire soon broke them and sent them fleeing across the field in

every direction. The infantry then retreated also. Advancing into the field, I halted near the middle of it, in doubt which direction to take. Just at that moment General Jackson came riding up from my rear alone. I reported my brigade as being solid, and asked for orders. My men recognised him and raised a terrific shout as he rode along the line with his hat off. He evidently knew how to appreciate a brigade that had gone through a hot battle and was then following retreating enemy without having broken its line of battle, and remained with me until the pursuit ceased.'

In stark contrast, General Crawford gave his own account of the flank movement made by his brigade:

'Onward these regiments charged, driving the enemy's infantry back through the wood beyond. But the reserves of the enemy were at once brought up and thrown upon the broken ranks. The field officers had been killed, wounded, or taken prisoners; the support I looked for did not arrive, and my gallant men, broken, decimated by that fearful fire, that unequal contest, fell back again across the space, leaving most of their number upon the field.'

The Confederates had already blocked General McClellan's Peninsular Campaign in the battles around Richmond in July. His troops were withdrawing. This fresh victory shifted the attentions from the Peninsula to Northern Virginia, and now General Lee's Confederates had the initiative and the upper hand.

Had Pope advanced in force with his whole command, then the situation might have been completely different. When Pope assumed command in person on 29 July, Banks was in Little Washington, Sigel at Sperryville and Ricketts's division of McDowell's Corps at Waterloo Bridge. In his defence, Pope was forced to move quickly for fear of Lee cutting him off from Washington. If McClellan's men had not taken time reinforcing Pope's new army, then the whole situation might have been completely different, and Cedar Mountain could well have been a crushing Confederate defeat.

Chapman's Mill (Thoroughfare Gap), 28 August 1862
Northern Virginia Campaign, June–September 1862

Union:
Brigadier-General James Ricketts
Army of Virginia III Corps, Second Division

Confederate:
Lieutenant-General James Longstreet
Army of Northern Virginia
Hood's Division
Whiting's Brigade

Thoroughfare Gap was a major route through the Bull Run mountains, and this action at Chapman's Mill ensured that Pope would be defeated at Second Manassas (29–30 August), as it allowed the two wings of Lee's army to unite.

On 28 August Jackson's Confederates were in grave danger of being surrounded by Pope's Union army. Pope's subordinate McDowell ordered Ricketts to move to Thoroughfare Gap and prevent Longstreet's troops from passing through the mountains and linking up with Jackson. Jackson had just raided the Union Supply Depot at Manassas Junction. Thoroughfare Gap had been held by King's Union Division, but now as Longstreet and Ricketts approached from the west and the east, it was unguarded.

Longstreet's troops were headed by Hood's Division, pushing skirmishers forward through the gap until they encountered Ricketts's artillery batteries covering the mouth. Hood continued to push his troops forward, threatening the flank of the batteries, but Union skirmishers initially held the ravine.

For some reason Ricketts ordered the batteries to withdraw. Almost simultaneously, Hood was ordered back to the gap. By the time that Longstreet ordered Hood forward again, Ricketts was gone, moving back towards Bristoe and then to Manassas Junction. By nightfall, Longstreet's men were streaming through

Thoroughfare Gap, grateful that Pope had not assigned a corps to the defence of the route, which would have undoubtedly stopped Longstreet in his tracks.

Sunrise found Longstreet's men marching towards Manassas, where Jackson was already engaged in an artillery duel. Jackson's men were formed up along an unfinished railway line running from Sudley Ford to Warrenton turnpike.

In Ricketts's defence, Confederate troops had passed through the mountains three miles to his north (at Hopewell Gap), which might have forced him to retire. Had his troops been thrown at Jackson's rear, Longstreet might have arrived too late to save his fellow general.

Casualties at Thoroughfare Gap were slight, perhaps no more than 100 between the two sides, but the significance of the encounter and the opportunities missed remain important.

Second Manassas (Second Bull Run), Virginia, 28–30 August 1862
Northern Virginia Campaign, June–September 1862

Union:
Major-General John Pope
Army of Virginia
Army of the Potomac
c.63,000 men
(total casualties c.13,830–14,462)

Confederate:
General Robert E. Lee
Army of Northern Virginia
c.47,000–54,000 men
(total casualties c.8,350–9,454)

Pope and Lee faced one another across the Rappahannock River. After the Battle of Cedar Mountain (9 August) Lee probed Pope's lines continually to find a weakness. He knew that he was fast running out of time, as when Fitzhugh Lee captured Pope's headquarters at Catlett's Station (22 August) he brought back with him the stunning news that McClellan's troops would arrive from the peninsula within five days.

Despite this bombshell, Lee still hoped to launch a decisive offensive against Pope. He intended to send half of his troops on a wide flanking manoeuvre to cut off the Union lines of communication. He would then follow, a day later, with the rest of his army. He knew that success depended on speed and precision, knowing that if he stayed and waited for Pope to attack, his army would be crushed.

Jackson and Stuart set off on the morning of 25 August with three days' rations. By that evening they had reached Salem, twenty-six miles away. The next

evening Jackson had reached Manassas, another thirty-six miles on, and had destroyed the Union supply depot. Jackson's move had not been ignored by Pope, who firmly believed that the Confederate was heading towards the valley. He also believed that Jackson's absence would make a victorious encounter with Lee all the more certain. Throughout the 25th Longstreet's Confederates continued to give all the signs that Lee's main army was still facing Pope, but on the evening of the 26th Pope discovered that Confederates were behind him. He was still sure that this was only a raid, but to make certain, he sent Sigel and McDowell to Gainesville. Porter and Banks would concentrate on Warrenton Junction and Reno, and Heintzelman would cover the gap at Greenwich and Bristoe Station. Whatever Confederates had managed to get around him were now, in Pope's mind, cut off. This Union move presented Pope with the ideal opportunity to destroy Jackson and his 24,000 men, whilst blocking Longstreet's 30,000.

Jackson, meanwhile, was still looking to find the ideal position on the Union flank. He needed to be able to hold out until Longstreet arrived. Initially he chose Stony Ridge, but was acutely aware that if he dug in then Pope could concentrate on his position and attack him before Longstreet arrived. Consequently he sent A.P. Hill towards Centreville and Ewell across Bull Run to meet Hill at Stony Ridge.

Pope was utterly confused and sent troops forward to try to pin down Jackson's men. When his troops arrived at Manassas on 28 August, the Confederates had gone. Pope then heard that Confederates were at Centreville and assumed that all of Jackson's 17

The 14th Brooklyn NY State Militia monument to Second Bull Run. The ridge is near where the battle opened (28 August 1862) and where Longstreet swooped down on Pope's Union troops in the flank two days later. (Malcolm Waddy III)

command was there. Consequently he ordered his whole army to proceed to Centreville at 16.15. By 17.30 King's Division, leading the Union move, was heading east on the Warrenton Turnpike when it came under fire.

The battle which ensued at Groveton resulted in high casualties on both sides, but Pope's men were concentrating on the area, and on 29 August Pope launched a series of assaults against Jackson. Some time between 11.00 and noon Longstreet arrived from Thoroughfare Gap. At the end of the day Jackson withdrew from his positions, and it seemed that Pope had no idea that Longstreet had arrived.

Looking from Jackson's line towards where Fitz John Porter's V Corps attacked on 30 August, just before they were crushed by Longstreet. Also where Berdan's sharpshooters fought at Second Bull Run. (Malcolm Waddy III)

On 30 August Pope renewed his attacks, but was faced by massed Confederate artillery that broke up his attacks. Longstreet counter-attacked with 28,000 men; it carried the whole of the Union left flank, and Pope's men were driven back to Bull Run.

As in the First Battle of Manassas, the house on Henry Hill was of great significance. Union troops, in holding this position, managed to cover Pope's retreat to Centreville across Bull Run, via the Stone Bridge.

The next day Lee continued his offensive and moved around the west of Centreville, hitting Fairfax Court House, whilst Jackson struck Union troops near Chantilly. This battle lasted until well into the evening, and Pope was forced to withdraw to the defences around Washington.

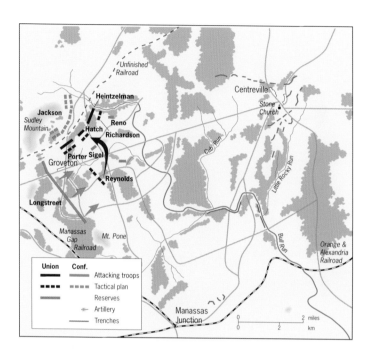

Harper's Ferry, West Virginia, 12–15 September 1862
The Maryland Campaign, 1862

Union:
Colonel Dixon S. Miles
c.13,000 men
(total casualties 12,419 captured, 44 killed, 173 wounded)

Confederate:
Major-General Thomas J. Jackson
c.2,300 men
(total casualties 39 killed, 247 wounded)

Stonewall Jackson's capture of Harper's Ferry resulted in the largest wholesale surrender of Union troops during the American Civil War, which still ranks as the third-largest surrender of US troops in American military history.

Under the direction of General Robert E. Lee, Jackson was sent rampaging up the lower Shenandoah Valley. He had just three days to clear the area for Lee before he launched his first major Confederate offensive into Union territory. Above all, it was Jackson's responsibility to prevent Union troops from disrupting Lee's supply lines and communications, whilst, at the same time, disrupting the enemy's own resources.

Jackson marched on Martinsburg and headed for the strategically important Harper's Ferry, which was a major junction on the Baltimore and Ohio railroad. Jackson deployed McLaws and Walker to cover the mountains overlooking Harper's Ferry on 14 September and then proceeded to bombard the Union garrison. During the night of the 14th 1,500 Union cavalry managed to escape, but the bombardment prompted Colonel Dixon Miles to surrender, though he died just minutes after raising the white flag. With Confederate artillery dominating the position from Maryland Heights, some 12,500 Union troops were forced to surrender.

Jackson marched into the town and paroled the prisoners, then he marched directly to Lee's aid at Antietam (Sharpsville), saving Lee from near-defeat. Some two months after, Union troops reoccupied Harper's Ferry, and this time they fortified the sur-

rounding heights that Jackson had used to such great effect. Harper's Ferry was later used as Sheridan's base in his own operations against Confederates in the Shenandoah Valley in 1864.

This victory, largely achieved by artillery fire, is notable for the fact that the majority of the Union guns were silenced in just two hours, from 15.00 to 17.00 on the 13th, and that the remaining Union artillery briefly returned fire on the 15th in the hour before the garrison surrendered at around 20.00.

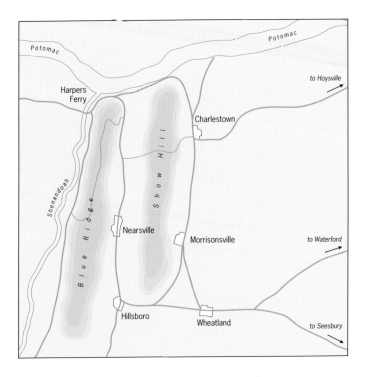

South Mountain (Boonsboro), Maryland, 14 September 1862
The Maryland Campaign, 1862

Union:
Major-General George B. McClellan
Army of the Potomac
c.30,000 men
(total casualties 1,813)

Confederate:
General Robert E. Lee
c.6,000 men
(total casualties unknown, but fewer than the Union)

Whilst Jackson was dealing with Union forces at Harper's Ferry, Lee was being pursued by McClellan

towards Frederick. Lee advanced on South Mountain and fought a series of pitched battles for possession of the South Mountain passes. Variously the Battle of South Mountain is also known as Crampton's Gap, Turner's Gap and Fox's Gap.

Fighting began when Confederate gunners in Fox's Gap and Turner's Gap opened fire on Union troops moving towards the mountain. Further south, at Crampton's Gap, Franklin's Union VI Corps moved from Jefferson but did not become engaged until around noon. He had wasted four hours considering his options, despite the fact that he outnumbered the Confederates ten to one.

When the Union assault did take place, they pushed the Confederates back up the mountain and through the gap. General Cobb's Confederates, some 1,300 strong, tried to hold the line, but in fifteen minutes 1,000 men were killed or wounded.

Following the clearing of Crampton's Gap, Franklin went into camp for the night. The Union forces missed the golden opportunity to pursue the Confederates and push a wedge between Lee's divided army. McClellan would then have had an opportunity to take on Lee piecemeal.

Having lost the battle at South Mountain, Lee ordered his men to converge on Sharpsburg. He did not discover until 16 September that Jackson had successfully taken Harper's Ferry

the day before. With Jackson on his way, Lee made the fatal decision to face McClellan at Antietam.

In many respects, although the Battle of South Mountain is often taken as being one engagement, the actions at Fox's Gap and Turner's Gap were very separate encounters from the action at Crampton's Gap. Collectively the action is significant, as the Union forces continued to labour under the false apprehension that the Confederates had deployed a large force to oppose them. In actual fact, until the late afternoon, there was only one weak Confederate division deployed.

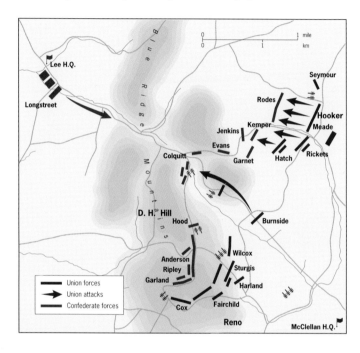

Antietam (Sharpsburg), 17 September 1862
Antietam Campaign, 1862

Union:
Major-General George B. McClellan
Army of the Potomac
6 infantry corps
1 cavalry division
195 infantry regiments, 14 cavalry regiments, 378 artillery pieces
c.87,000 men
(total casualties 12,410: 2,108 killed, 9,549 wounded and 753 captured or missing)

Confederate:
General Robert E. Lee
Army of Northern Virginia
Longstreet's Corps
Jackson's Corps
Reserve artillery
Cavalry division
186 infantry regiments, 15 cavalry regiments, 292 artillery pieces
c.40,000 men
(total casualties 11,172: 1,512 killed, 7,816 wounded, 1,844 captured or missing)

On 5 May 1862 Lee's Army of Northern Virginia crossed the Potomac River to invade the North. He hoped to bring the war to the Northern states which had, so far, been spared the

destruction that Virginia had been forced to endure. Lee estimated that it would take the Union commander, McClellan, at least two weeks to move on him.

21

By 7 September Lee was concentrating his forces around Frederick, Maryland. From there he sent Jackson to capture Harper's Ferry. Meanwhile, McClellan had already reacted and was moving cautiously to cover Washington and find Lee's army. At Frederick, Lee authorised Special Order No. 191, the blueprint for his invasion plan.

In the plan he sought to split his army into five parts; Jackson's move against Harper's Ferry was the first stage. Longstreet would advance towards the Pennsylvania border, whilst D.H. Hill would be positioned at South Mountain to prevent Union troops escaping from Harper's Ferry. Each of the commanders was given a copy of the detailed plan, but one copy went missing. The Confederate rearguard left Frederick on 12 September, harassed by lead elements of the Union army. As the liberated town rejoiced when Union soldiers marched in, a copy of the order was found in Lee's abandoned headquarters. In hours it was in McClellan's hands.

McClellan's troops headed for South Mountain, aiming to split the Confederate army and defeat it in detail. All that stood in McClellan's way were some Confederate cavalry and D.H. Hill's division. Meanwhile, Lee's plan had fallen behind schedule: the troops were converging on Harper's Ferry, but they had only driven in the Union outposts.

Lee now heard of what had become of the last copy of his plans, and accordingly ordered Longstreet back to South Mountain to support D.H. Hill. On the morning of 14 September Union troops began their assault on Hill's positions, Longstreet's men arrived and the Confederates held until nightfall.

On the night of the 14th the Confederates firmed up their stranglehold on Harper's Ferry. At dawn, their artillery fired for just an hour before the Union troops surrendered.

Lee now hoped to reconsolidate his forces at Sharpsburg and face McClellan. He positioned his army along the four-mile front with both flanks resting on the Potomac River. The only fear was that if the line were to be broken, there was just one ford across which his army could retreat.

McClellan's army duly arrived at noon on 15 September. Jackson arrived on the 16th and took command of the left flank of the Confederate army. McClellan planned to attack at 14.00, but due to delays there was only an artillery barrage and some skirmishing by Hooker's I Corps on Jackson's front.

At 06.00 on 17 September Hooker's Union soldiers marched down the Hagerstown Turnpike, and Doubleday and Ricketts advanced, encountering Confederates hidden in the Cornfield. Preceded by a hail of artillery fire, the Cornfield was captured, allowing Union troops to occupy the East and West Woods.

Jackson's troops counter-attacked, supported by D.H. Hill and Hood, and pushed the Union troops right back to their own artillery positions. Here, the Confederates were repelled with the massed guns. Now the Union XII Corps arrived, under the command of Mansfield, at 59 the oldest general in the Union army. His appearance was short-lived, as he was shot near the East Woods. His command was taken by Alpheus Williams. Jackson's men cut down the new commander's troops, but the other half of his corps had reached Dunker Church. Here the Union corps could neither advance nor fall back for several hours.

The Confederate left was in peril, but Jackson had stopped the Union attack in its tracks. In the centre, the Union II Corps eventually moved forward,

22   *Burnside Bridge as seen from the Confederate position on the heights above at Antietam. (Malcolm Waddy III)*

straight into the West Woods area where Jackson was waiting for him. The tightly packed Union columns were slaughtered, and in twenty minutes over 2,500 were killed or wounded.

Shortly after 09.00, French's division of II Corps pushed back the Confederate outpost at Roulette Farm and advanced down the slope to the Sunken Road. Here they encountered two of D.H. Hill's brigades, who hit the Union troops time and time again with measured and devastating volleys.

As French's men reeled from the fire, Longstreet broke through their lines with 4,000 men, capturing Roulette Farm. Here they were counter-attacked by Meagher's Irish Brigade, mostly Irish immigrants from New York. With the support of the last of II Corps, they swept the Confederates back to the Sunken Road.

At the crucial point when the Confederates should have contested the Sunken Road, the 6th Alabama pulled out. The result was disastrous, leaving the Confederate flank exposed. The slaughter of Confederates in this area led to it being renamed 'Bloody Lane'.

The Union troops were now in the heart of the Confederate line, all of Lee's reserves had been committed and only a desperate charge by Hill dissuaded the Union troops from pushing forward.

In order to exploit the weaknesses in the Confederate centre, McClellan now brought up 25,000 fresh troops. Three Union corps had been broken, and at this crucial time McClellan chose not to commit his last reserves.

A third assault was about to take place, with Burnside's IX Corps attacking across the Lower Bridge on the Antietam. It was held by just 450 Confederates under Toombs. Between 10.00 and 13.00 Burnside tried to dislodge Toombs, and eventually 10,000 men passed over the narrow bridge. It was not until 15.00 that IV Corps finally hit the Confederate main line. It was too late: A.P. Hill's men had marched 17 miles and by 16.30 had pushed Burnside back to the creek. Nothing more could be achieved that day. Lee was all for counter-attacking in the morning, but agreed to wait for McClellan to act first. McClellan, meanwhile, wary that the Confederates had been reinforced, also decided to wait for Lee.

During the night of the 18th Lee crossed the Potomac at Shepardstown. Lee had been stopped: although he wanted to fight, his casualties had ripped the heart out of his army.

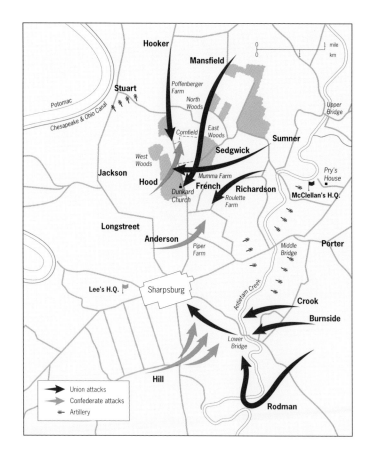

23

Fredericksburg (Marye's Heights), Virginia, 11–15 December 1862

The Fredericksburg Campaign, November–December 1862

Union:
Major-General Ambrose E. Burnside
Army of the Potomac
*c.*116,683 men
(total casualties 13,353)

Confederate:
General Robert E. Lee
Army of Northern Virginia
*c.*72,497 men
(total casualties 4,576)

Burnside sent a corps of his Army of the Potomac to occupy Falmouth, near Fredericksburg on 14 October 1862. Having established a presence, the rest of his army followed, but Robert E. Lee's Army of Northern Virginia responded by digging in on the heights around Fredericksburg, dominating the entire area.

Under heavy fire, Union engineers on 11 December erected five pontoon bridges across the Rappahannock River. On the following day, Burnside's army streamed across to deploy, directly opposing the Confederate defence works. On 13 December Burnside ordered a series of frontal assaults against Marye's Heights and Prospect Hill. They were all beaten off with huge casualties. The only penetration of the Confederate defence works was made by Meade's men, who managed to break through Jackson's line, but were swiftly driven back by a Confederate counter-attack. The main Union assault on that day was led by Hooker, whose task it was to capture Marye's Heights. As a Confederate officer noted at the time, it was a suicidal strategy:

'The enemy, having deployed, now showed himself above the crest of the ridge and advanced in columns of brigades, and at once our guns began their deadly work with shell

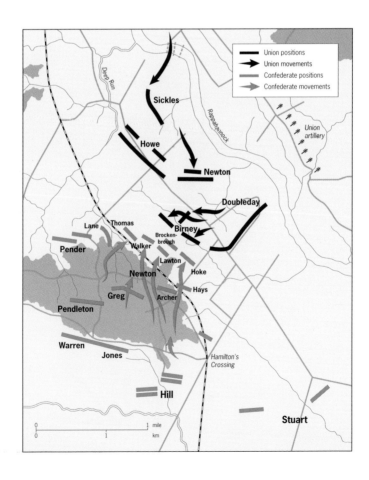

and solid shot. How beautifully they came on. Their bright bayonets glistering in the sunlight made the line look like a huge serpent of blue and steel. The very force of their onset levelled the broad fences bounding the small fields and gardens that interspersed the plain. We could see our shells bursting in their ranks, making great gaps; but on they came, as though they would go straight through and over us. Now we gave them canister, and that staggered them. A few more paces onward and the Georgians in the road below us rose up, and, glancing an instant along their rifle barrels, let loose a storm of lead into the faces of the advance brigade. This was too much; the column hesitated, and then turning, took refuge behind the bank.'

In the assaults Union Generals Jackson and Bayard were killed, along with the Confederate Generals Cobb and Maxey Gregg.

The assault had gone in at noon following a Union bombardment. Meade's success occurred in a marshy area around 13.00. At 13.30 Gibbon was sent to support Meade, but by 14.15 Meade had been driven out of his breakthrough. By 14.30 the Union troops were in full retreat. However, they had sufficient fight left in them to fend off a Confederate counter-attack which was launched at 15.00.

On 15 December Burnside decided to call off the assault on Fredericksburg, and he recrossed the Rappahannock River. This effectively ended the cam-

paign, but in January 1863 Burnside started a new offensive, which was an abject failure. This new campaign, now referred to as the Mud March, led to Burnside being replaced by Major-General Joseph Hooker later in January 1863.

In Burnside's defence, he had moved steadily towards Richmond and planned on making a rapid crossing of the Rappahannock in order to seize Fredericksburg. He knew that in seizing the town and occupying the surrounding heights, he would be able to hold off almost anything that Lee could throw at him. In the event, the pontoon bridges that Burnside so desperately needed took seventeen days to arrive. In those vital days Lee had plenty of time to prepare his defences for the inevitable assault that Burnside would have to deliver to capture the heights around Fredericksburg. The preparatory bombardment on 11 December which reduced much of Fredericksburg to ashes, and the covering fire provided by the Union artillery for the actual crossing, failed to dislodge Confederate snipers, who continually delayed the engineers' efforts to finish the pontoons. When Burnside was ready to launch his assault on Lee's lines, well-placed Confederate artillery broke up both Franklin's assault, south of the town, and Hooker's attempt to take Marye's Heights. Burnside threw seven Union divisions against Marye's Heights, and each time they were stopped in their tracks.

At the end of the battle thousands of Union troops were left dying on the battlefield. They lay there all night before medical aid was given to them the following day. By then many more had died.

The railroad line that was present during the Battle of Fredericksburg, seen from the southern end of Prospect Hill.
(Malcolm Waddy III)

25

Union:
Major-General Joseph Hooker
Army of the Potomac
7 infantry corps
2 cavalry corps
274 infantry regiments, 27 cavalry regiments,
404 artillery pieces
*c.*140,000 men (97,382 engaged)
(total casualties 14,000)

Confederate:
General Robert E. Lee
Army of Northern Virginia
$1\frac{1}{2}$ infantry corps
Cavalry divisions
110 infantry regiments, 22 cavalry regiments,
232 artillery pieces
*c.*65,000 men (57,352 engaged)
(total casualties 10,000)

Thomas Jonathan 'Stonewall' Jackson.

The morale of the Army of the Potomac had vastly improved with the elevation of 'Fighting Joe' Hooker to commander. He replaced the ill-fated Burnside, who had in turn replaced McClellan.

Hooker's resources were vast yet disorganised, and seemingly important to provide the victory that the North, Lincoln and Washington craved. He set about reforming the army with a vengeance, forming a cavalry corps and a reliable scouting network. Above all, the Union army had always suffered from not being in the right place at the right time to use its overwhelming numbers.

There was also an opportunity to strike at Lee at this time. A considerable number of Lee's men had been detailed under Longstreet and were in the Suffolk area. Leaving a substantial force at Fredericksburg, Hooker's army crossed the Rapidan and Rappahannock Rivers leading west. Hooker dispatched cavalry to raid Lee's lines of supply and communications with Richmond. In doing this he assumed that Lee would have to turn and deal with this threat, and in doing so he would trap Lee and defeat him.

By 29 April, Hooker's cavalry and three of his infantry corps had crossed Kelly's Ford, with the cavalry pushing west and the infantry marching to capture the Getmanna and Ely Fords. On the 30th, the vast Union columns rejoined one another at Chancellorsville.

Lee, meanwhile, had received the alarming news of Union troop movements in the Wilderness area. Hooker had surprised him by his daring march, which had passed right in front of the Confederates' noses.

Immediately Lee sent Anderson's Division to find out exactly where the Union troops were, and, if possible, where they were heading. Anderson found them at Chancellorsville and began digging trench works around the Zoan Church area. Lee then sent up Stonewall Jackson to reinforce, his command arriving to help block the Union passage on 1 May.

As the day progressed, more Union troops arrived at Chancellorsville, until nearly 115,000 men were massed in the area. Hooker had, however, misjudged Lee. His adversary had no intention of retreating on Richmond; already he was sending orders for his own men to converge on the Union army. Although Lee was outnumbered, he was determined to deal with Hooker's army.

Leaving a part of his army to cover Fredericksburg, the rest of Lee's forces headed west towards Chancellorsville. The lead elements encountered Union troops on 1 May; Hooker ordered his troops to pull back on Chancellorsville. Hooker hoped that Lee was not expecting him to be there in so great a force and that the Confederates would push through the dense woodland and stumble on his troops. In this way, Hooker thought, Lee's men could be defeated piecemeal as they blundered, uncoordinated and ill-prepared into his lines.

Lee, however, was too wily a bird to be caught out like this. Accordingly he detached two divisions to give the impression that he was falling into Hooker's trap, whilst he detached the bulk of his army under Stonewall Jackson west. Jackson would have to pass near the Union front and position himself on the vulnerable right flank of the Union army.

Jackson's troops marched solidly through the morning and afternoon of 2 May, arriving in positions just two hours before dusk. No sooner had his men taken up positions than they fell on Howard's Union XI Corps. Jackson's men routed Howard's men, but in the gathering darkness, he was forced to halt his attacks in order to regroup his forces.

This is the site of the Wilderness Tavern dependency. General Thomas Jackson had his arm amputated near here at the battle of Chancellorsville. (Malcolm Waddy III)

Ever keen to press on, Jackson rode out beyond the front line, eager to discover where the enemy lay. Unfortunately, one of his own pickets shot him by mistake and he was carried from the battlefield mortally wounded. Later that night, his left arm was amputated below the shoulder. Jackson would die on 10 May whilst recuperating from pneumonia.

Lee appointed J.E.B. Stuart, the cavalry commander, as Jackson's successor on the field, and on 3 May the Confederates resumed their assault. It was to be the bloodiest day of the battle as Stuart's men fought to break through to be reunited with Lee's troops. By now Hooker had regained control of the army, and the Confederates found the Union troops far more prepared and willing to fight. Hooker had withdrawn to the north of Chancellor House, with the Confederates closing in for the final battle.

Union guns situated at Chancellorsville with Hazel Grove in the distance. (Malcolm Waddy III)

The Stonewall Jackson monument is located near the Visitor Centre at Chancellorsville. (Malcolm Waddy III)

Unexpected news saved Hooker's army. Lee received a despatch from Jubal Early that Union troops had broken through his lines at Fredericksburg and were heading for him. Lee organised a line at Salem Church, which forced the Union troops to retreat across the Rappahannock River. Content with this action, Lee now discovered to his horror that Hooker had abandoned Chancellorsville and his troops had almost crossed the Rappahannock.

Hooker's retreat had nearly been a disaster when storms almost wrecked the pontoons across the Rappahannock. At the same time, however, the storms had masked his move from Confederate eyes.

Lee had won the battle, defeated Hooker and the Army of the Potomac once again, but he had failed to take the very real opportunity to annihilate it.

In effect, Chancellorsville was an empty victory; nothing had come of the battle strategically or militarily. The battle hastened the removal of Hooker from commanding the Army of the Potomac, but had dealt a heavy blow to the Confederacy. They and Lee had lost the South's most capable and ferocious general in Stonewall Jackson; he could not be replaced.

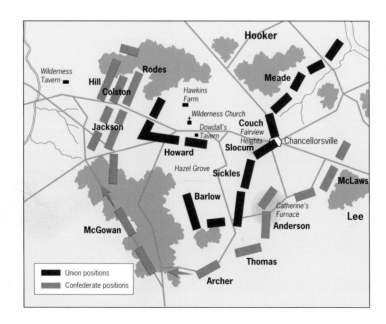

Winchester (Second battle), Virginia 13–15 June 1863

Gettysburg Campaign, June–August 1863

Union:
Brigadier-General Robert Milroy
c.7,000 men
(total casualties 4,443)

Confederate:
Lieutenant-General Richard S. Ewell
c.12,500 men
(total casualties 266)

Following the Battle of Brandy Station on 9 June 1863, General Robert E. Lee ordered Lieutenant-General Ewell and his II Corps of the Army of Northern Virginia into the Shenandoah, with the instructions to clear the valley of Union troops. Lee and Ewell were well aware of the fact that Brigadier-General Milroy was in strength at Winchester.

Ewell arrived supported by Early's and Edward Johnson's divisions on the evening of 13 June. Telling Early the following day to lead a brigade south of the town, Ewell moved his main force to the north-western side, seizing the outposts, including West Fort (which was taken by the Louisiana Brigade), and he ordered Johnson to deploy east of the town.

Ewell launched an assault at around 18.00 on the 14th and drove the Union troops out of the defence works and into the town itself. Milroy considered he had no other option than to retreat and abandon his artillery and supplies. Ewell, aware that this might be his enemy's only option, sent Johnson to occupy the Martinsburg Pike north of the town. Johnson carried out the flanking march before daylight and positioned his troops at Stephenson's Depot. As Milroy began his retreat at 02.00 on the 15th, his men got only two miles before they were blocked by Johnson. There was a pitched battle as Milroy's men desperately tried to break through. Some managed to reach Harper's Ferry and others fled to Hancock on the Potomac River, but the vast majority were captured.

Ewell was able to report to Lee that he had captured 4,000 Union infantry, 28 artillery pieces, 300 wagons and a vast quantity of ammunition and supplies. This victory at Winchester provided Lee with the opportunity of launching his second invasion of the North.

By the 15th Ewell had also crossed the Potomac and had occupied Hagerstown and Sharpsburg, and had sent Jenkins's cavalry to Chambersburg to collect supplies. The Union responded by withdrawing the Harper's Ferry garrison on the 17th.

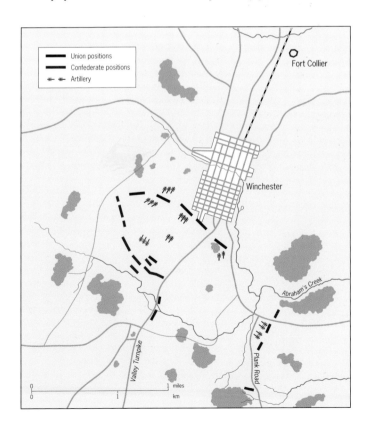

29

Union:
Major-General George G. Meade
Army of the Potomac
240 infantry regiments
31 cavalry regiments
370 guns
c.83,289–85,500 men
(total casualties 23,049)

Confederate:
General Robert E. Lee
Army of Northern Virginia
168 infantry regiments
27 cavalry regiments
287 artillery pieces
c.75,054 men
(total casualties 27–28,000)

For the second time in a year Robert E. Lee decided to invade the North. His army had reached a manpower peak. Lee's plan was to advance north and pick a spot where they would stand and let the Union army destroy itself in attacking them. Lee moved his troops north-west along the Blue Ridge Mountains, leaving A.P. Hill to hold the positions in front of Richmond. Lee's movement was shielded by Stuart's 10,000-strong cavalry corps.

On the morning of 9 June Union cavalry commander Pleasanton crossed the Rappahannock River near Stuart's headquarters and engaged Stuart in a running battle on the river plain. Although Pleasanton lost the battle, Washington was now sure that Lee had left the Richmond area.

Hooker, as commander of the Army of the Potomac, was ordered to make a parallel march following Lee's columns as they travelled north, in case the Confederates turned to move on Washington.

The Confederates overran the Union troops at Winchester on 14 June, capturing 5,000 men and 200,000 rounds of ammunition. Lee's main force crossed the Potomac River near Sharpsburg, and Washington was forced to mobilise 37,000 men from Pennsylvania and Ohio.

By 27 June the Union army had only reached Frederick, Maryland, when Hooker was told that he had been replaced by Meade. Meade immediately increased the pace of the march, and as Lee moved north, so did the Union troops. By now the Confederates were deep into Pennsylvania and Stuart was riding around at will, capturing Union detachments and supplies.

Lee now concentrated around Cashtown, and was proceeding towards Gettysburg, near the Maryland border. On 30 June Union cavalry arrived in Gettysburg. The commander, Buford, was assured

Little Round Top from Warren Avenue. (Lisa Mattson)

View looking north from Little Round Top. (Lisa Mattson)

that Reynolds's I Corps would arrive by late morning. Consequently Buford deployed his men on McPherson's Ridge to delay the Confederates. The Confederate advance was led by A.P. Hill, who believed that Gettysburg was only held by local militia. He gave permission for Heth to move into the town and liberate a large consignment of shoes. On the morning of 1 July Heth's men arrived and ran into Buford's skirmishers. More Confederates were arriving, but Reynolds's Union troops had kept their promise and had also arrived.

Reynolds was shot dead by a Confederate sharpshooter, and Doubleday, one of Reynolds's divisional commanders, took over and sent an urgent message to Meade. Buford and I Corps were holding the line well, and were soon joined by Howard's XI Corps, who took up position above the town.

The Confederates seized Oak Hill and from there concentrated on the junction between the two Union corps. Lee suddenly arrived on the battlefield and was appalled to find Hill's men already in battle. He ordered them to wait until Longstreet and the rest of the army could arrive.

Rodes had already launched an attack on the junction of the two Union corps, and the Union right was collapsing. Lee changed his mind and sent Heth and Pender to launch a frontal assault on McPherson's Ridge. The Union troops streamed back to Cemetery Hill where Hancock and his II

Corps had just arrived. He took command of the battle and sent men to hold Culp's Hill to the east. Later in the afternoon Slocum's XII Corps also arrived, and the battle line was fixed along Cemetery Ridge.

During the night both sides brought up fresh reinforcements. Meade was sure that the position was a good one, and despite Lee's initial reticence of fighting a major engagement here, he, too, decided it was a good place to fight.

By noon on 2 July all but the Union VI Corps and Pickett's Confederates had arrived. Lee's plan was to send Longstreet round to the right, across the Emmitsburg Road and attack Cemetery Ridge from the flank. Whilst Longstreet was manoeuvring, the Union III Corps under Sickles advanced towards the Peach Orchard. His command was spread perilously thin and did not rest to the right of the existing Union line. Meade rode out to stop him but it was too late; before he could withdraw his troops, Hood and McLaws swung around his left wing and surged over the heavily wooded area called Round Top.

The swift action of Vincent's brigade meant that Union troops got to Little Round Top before the Confederates. Vincent was supported by a battery of guns which bore down on Devil's Den, a boulder-strewn area that changed hands several times. Meade was forced to throw brigade after brigade into the Wheatfield area and Devil's Den. Longstreet now hit

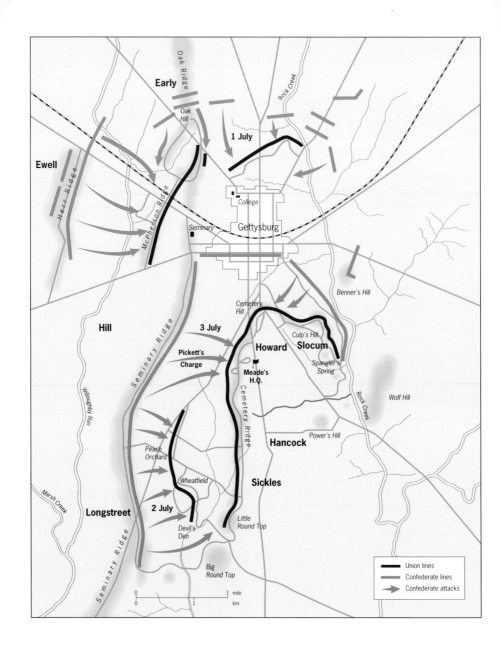

Map labels:

Oak Ridge
Early
Oak Hill
Rock Creek
1 July
Ewell
Herr Ridge
McPherson Ridge
College
Seminary
Gettysburg
Benner's Hill
Cemetery Hill
Hill
Seminary Ridge
3 July
Culp's Hill
Howard
Slocum
Pickett's Charge
Spangler's Spring
Meade's H.Q.
Willoughby Run
Cemetery Ridge
Rock Creek
Wolf Hill
Power's Hill
Hancock
Peach Orchard
Wheatfield
Sickles
Marsh Creek
Longstreet
2 July
Devil's Den
Little Round Top
Seminary Ridge
Big Round Top

0 ___ 1 mile
0 ___ 1 km

— Union lines
— Confederate lines
→ Confederate attacks

---

the Wheatfield and the Peach Orchard, puncturing the Union front. Isolated Union units fought on and the whole of the Union left flank was in grave danger. Units from the Union III Corps moved to the left flank to stem the Confederate attack. Sedgwick's men, who had just arrived, moved in, and this proved to be the deciding moment: the Confederates began to fall back, although fighting in Devil's Den continued until late in the evening.

Elsewhere Johnston had failed to take Culp's Hill because of the well-placed Union gun batteries, and Early's assault on Cemetery Hill had been held by Howard, but finally broke and had to be reinforced by Hancock. As the fighting ceased for the night,

Meade judged correctly that the next assault would be on his centre. The Union centre was arrayed along Cemetery Ridge, and at 13.00 15,000 Confederates under Pickett aimed to burst through the Union line. Longstreet was set against the plan from the beginning, and said:

'I have been a soldier all my life. I have been with soldiers engaged in fights by couples, squads, companies, regiments, divisions and armies, and I should know as well as anyone what soldiers can do. It is my opinion that no 15,000 men ever arrayed for battle can take that position.'

McPherson Farm. (Lisa Mattson)

The Trostle House. (Lisa Mattson)

The 15,000 would face 5,500 Union troops supported by 170 guns. The Confederate batteries opened up first and for two hours they ripped into one another's lines. Shortly afterwards Pickett's men marched forward, and at 300 yards Union skirmishers picked off Confederate officers, but Pickett was gathering speed, advancing at 100 yards a minute. They were hit by four successive lines of rifles and close-range canister-shot. Men were falling all around, but 150 men burst through the wall of steel, though they were quickly overwhelmed. Pickett was outnumbered and out-gunned, his charge a dreadful act of bravado. Of the 15,000, just 5,000 made it back to the Confederate lines.

Lee rode to help rally Pickett's men, fearing a counter-attack. He took off his hat and rode amongst them begging their forgiveness and urging them to re-form. Pickett joined him. He had been bottom of his class at West Point, but was assured of his place in history for all of the wrong reasons. Lee told him to re-form his men, to which Pickett replied, 'General Lee, I have no division.' Lee simply answered, 'Come, General Pickett, this has been my fight and upon my shoulders rests the blame.'

Meanwhile, three miles to the rear of the Union army, Stuart's Confederates had appeared and were charged by four successive Michigan cavalry regiments, led by Brigadier-General George Armstrong Custer. Although this cavalry battle was inconclusive, Stuart could not fall on the enemy's rear, and had to ride round to rejoin Lee.

Following Pickett's charge the Confederate army was all but exhausted, but the Union troops had no stomach or energy to mount a counter-attack. Equally, the whole defensive perimeter was a jumble of units, and corps had become mixed. The two armies continued to face one another during 4 July, Independence Day, but that night Lee finally acknowledged defeat and began a steady withdrawal to the south.

The overall casualties were enormous, with over 50,000 killed, wounded, missing or captured. Lee's hope for a decisive battle had ended in failure, but had prevented the threat of a Union invasion of Virginia. Despite the failure and the appalling casualties, the Confederates' spirit was not broken, and as one survivor of Pickett's charge told Lee: 'We'll fight them Sir, till hell freezes over, and then we'll fight them on the ice.'

Bristoe Station, Virginia, 14 October 1863
Union Offensive after Gettysburg, 1863

Union:
Major-General G.K. Warren
II Corps, Army of the Potomac
546 casualties

Confederate:
Lieutenant-General A.P. Hill
Heth's and Anderson's Divisions
1,378 casualties

After Gettysburg (1–3 July 1863), Union forces pressed the retreating Confederates until Lee turned to fight at Beaver Creek (10 July). The engagement was inconclusive and Lee fell back on Funkstown on 12 July, again falling back across the Potomac when Union forces closed in.

Meade's Union Army of the Potomac crossed the river in pursuit, establishing his headquarters at Culpepper Court House on 13 September. By October, however, Lee was back on the offensive, pushing Meade back towards Centreville. His advance forces of A.P. Hill's III Corps collided with the retreating enemy at the railroad embankment at Bristoe Station on 14 October. Meade had posted Warren's II Corps along the Orange and Alexandria railroad. As the Confederates advanced, they came under heavy fire from Warren's men in their concealed positions.

Heth's division, led by Cooke's and Kirkland's brigades, were repulsed with heavy losses, losing a battery of five guns in the process. Lee had not expected to encounter the enemy line here, and despite A.P. Hill's best efforts, he could not dislodge Warren.

The Union army was therefore able to retreat back towards Centreville, without being harassed by Lee. In effect, this blunted Lee's Bristoe offensive. The Confederates had to be content with tearing up the Orange and Alexandria railroad and a slow retirement to the Rappahannock River. This was destined to be Lee's last major offensive of the war in Northern Virginia.

As for Hill, he lost the respect of Lee owing to the reverse, and Lee ordered him to bury the dead and never to mention Bristoe Station again.

Meade reorganised at Centreville; he then pressed Lee, rebuilding the railroad as he advanced. There was a collision at Gainesville on 19 October, but this was simply a holding action on the part of Lee, as by the 20th Meade was firmly established at Warrentown. For some time, the two armies would face one another across the Rappahannock and Rapidan Rivers until a major new Union offensive on 7 November. By late November, Lee would be fighting desperately in the heart of Virginia against an increasingly overwhelming Union army.

Union:
Major-General Ulysses S. Grant
Army of the Potomac
c.101,895 men (plus cavalry)
(total casualties 17,666)

Confederate:
General Robert E. Lee
Army of Northern Virginia
c.61,025 men
(total casualties c.7,750)

On 4 May the Army of the Potomac crossed the Rappahannock River on another determined invasion of the South. By the afternoon Hancock's corps had arrived at Chancellorsville, Warren's Corps was at the Old Wilderness Tavern and Union cavalry were thrown out ahead.

Lee had been fully apprised for a number of days that Grant's army, led by Meade, would be heading in this direction, and he knew that the enemy had to traverse the very difficult Wilderness terrain. Lee determined to hit Grant at the earliest opportunity, and his various commands were converging.

At 18.00 on 4 May Grant issued orders that the march should continue south-east at 05.00 the following day. By 07.15 on the 5th, Warren's troops had encountered Confederates located about two miles from the Wilderness Tavern. Grant believed that the Confederates could be of no more than divisional strength. At around noon Warren's men advanced, but despite initial successes they were counter-attacked and driven back. Fresh Union troops arrived at around 15.00, just in time to hold back a fresh

Confederate counter-attack. Unfortunately for Warren, on his other flank the Confederates had pushed through a gap and managed to rout advancing Union reinforcements. Further to the south, Union cavalry on the Plank Road held Parker's Store, whilst more went south-west towards Craig's Meeting House. Elements of A.P. Hill's Confederates surged up the Plank Road and drove the Union troops towards Wilderness Tavern. Fresh Union infantry were sent to stop this advance, and Hancock's Corps concentrated around Todd's Tavern. Hancock had already been given orders to advance, and was actually two miles beyond the tavern, near Shady Grove Church, and had to withdraw. The Union infantry had managed to stop A.P. Hill's men, and more troops arrived at 14.00 to consolidate the position. Both sides were digging in, and Hancock dug in just in the nick of time before he was attacked at 16.15. The fighting here was desperate, with charges and counter-charges until around 17.30. Eventually Hill's men were driven back several hundred yards, but A.P. Hill's 14,000 had held 38,000 men. Hill had expected Longstreet's men to support him, but they did not arrive until late in the evening.

Grant, meanwhile, moved up Burnside's Corps during the night to reinforce Hancock, and had ordered a general assault at dawn on 6 May. Longstreet and Anderson likewise arrived to reinforce A.P. Hill. At 05.00 Union troops advanced, making some inroads into Hill's line. All seemed lost for the Confederates until elements of Longstreet's corps arrived to support them. Gibbon's Union troops on the south flank, along Brock Road, began to advance, running into stiff opposition from the Confederates. Shortly before 09.00 Hancock

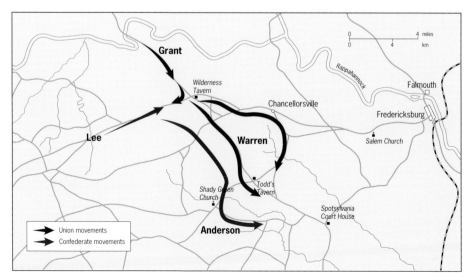

This is Ellwood, which served as the Union V Corps headquarters during the Wilderness Campaign. (Malcolm Waddy III)

resumed his advance along the Plank Road, whilst Sheridan's cavalry fought Stuart's Confederate horsemen at Todd's Tavern. Burnside's men had not moved up onto Hancock's right, and consequently, without his support, Longstreet had pushed Hancock back by 09.45.

Longstreet decided to attack the Union south flank, and at 11.00, after fierce fighting, the Union line was withdrawn to the Brock Road. Around this time Longstreet was shot by one of his own men, just five miles from where Stonewall Jackson had suffered a similar fate almost a year before.

Burnside was finally in position at around 16.00, and attacked near the Tapp House, but was driven back. The Confederates now counter-attacked, and although the Union line held for around half an hour, the Confederates carried the line. Fresh Union

counter-attacks pushed the Confederates back once more.

In the north Sedgwick and Warren faced Ewell, and at 17.30 the Confederates fell on Sedgwick's exposed right flank. The Confederates burst through, capturing several hundred men, as well as Generals Shaler and Seymour. Eventually fresh Union infantry pushed them back out of the defences.

By mutual consent the wounded were collected on 7 May following a number of brush fires which threatened to incinerate the incapacitated men. In fact some two hundred men were suffocated or burned to death on the night of 7/8 May because of brush fires.

Under the cover of darkness Grant's forces withdrew, to meet again at Spotsylvania.

Spotsylvania, Virginia, 8–21 May 1864
The Wilderness Campaign, 1864

Union:
Lieutenant-General Ulysses S. Grant
Major-General George G. Meade
Army of the Potomac
237 infantry regiments
35 cavalry regiments
274 artillery pieces
c.111,000 men (actual effectives *c*.90,000)
(total casualties 18,399)

Confederate:
General Robert E. Lee
Army of Northern Virginia
164 infantry regiments
25 cavalry regiments
200 artillery pieces
c.63,000 men (actual effectives *c*.50,000)
(total casualties *c*.10,000)

These are the trenches that were reconstructed during 2000 to demonstrate what they looked like during the Battle of Spotsylvania. (Malcolm Waddy III)

Grant had taken command of the entire Union army in March 1864. He found that there were 860,000 men on the muster rolls, but of these only 533,000 were fit for duty. The vast majority of these men were assigned to backwater posts, now of little strategic use. Grant set about reorganising and reinforcing the Army of the Potomac. He knew that the North had an overwhelming superiority in men and material, and proposed to use it to crush Lee.

His first battle against Lee during the Wilderness Campaign had ended inconclusively, with both sides claiming the victory. As far as Grant was concerned, his loss of nearly 18,000 men was a fair trade for Lee's more proportionate loss of 8,000.

At 06.00 on 7 May Grant issued an order to the commander of the Army of the Potomac, Meade, to 'Make all preparations during the day for a night march to take position at Spotsylvania Court House.' During the night of 7/8 May the Union V Corps and Anderson's Confederate I Corps were both heading for the same destination. They encountered one another on the Brock Road at Spindle Farm, with

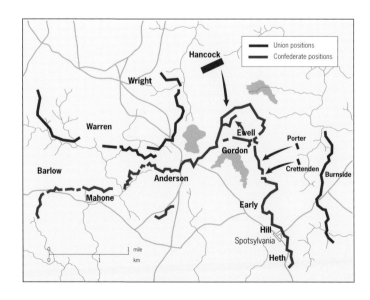

This monument marks the approximate location of where Major-General John Sedgwick was killed by Confederate sharp-shooters during the battle of Spotsylvania. (Malcolm Waddy III)

both sides feeding new troops in during the day. The arrival of Sedgwick's VI Corps allowed the Union troops to force their way forward, only to find more fieldworks blocking their way.

More troops arrived on both sides during 9 May. Early's Confederates occupied Spotsylvania Court House, and the Union II Corps under Hancock moved to support the right of Warren's V Corps. The Confederate positions, which later became known as 'The Mule Shoe', resembled an enormous inverted 'V'. Anderson's troops straddled the Brock Road, Ewell's men occupied the centre and Early the long flank which edged down towards Spotsylvania Court House. As it would turn out, the bulk of the fighting would happen on the triangular salient a mile long and half a mile wide. Ewell had fortified it with abatis, gun platforms and rifle pits. The mule shoe would face its first major test in the early evening of 10 May.

For the whole day Grant had been probing to find a weakness, and the following day was taken up with Grant manoeuvring three of his four army corps around the mule shoe. That night, fearing a massive Union offensive, Lee ordered Ewell to retire his artillery pieces to the main lines. This was to be a fatal mistake.

At 04.40 20,000 Union troops of Hancock's corps burst onto Ewell's line. The attack totally overwhelmed the Confederates and over 2,000 were captured. Hancock pushed in towards Lee's only reserves but was stopped. The Confederates now counter-attacked and by mid-morning the Union

troops had been driven back almost to the original Confederate line.

At 06.00 Wright had tried, without success, to attack an area on the north-west face of the mule shoe, called Bloody Angle. He had been driven back with huge losses. At 09.15 Warren had tried to push Anderson from the Brock Road, and again had met with little success. Finally Grant threw in Burnside at 16.00 but the battle was being won or lost in the desperate struggle with Hancock's corps. Lee managed to secure the line, with both sides backing off to reconsider. It was not until 18 May that Grant again hurled Hancock against the Confederate lines.

On 19 May the Confederates discovered fresh Union troops coming up from Washington. Ewell's men rushed to meet them at Harris Farm, where both sides suffered huge casualties.

The two armies finally left Spotsylvania on 20 and 21 May. Lee headed south towards Richmond. Grant had failed to defeat or destroy the Army of Northern Virginia. As far as Lee was concerned, he had managed to delay Grant for two weeks, but strategically both the Wilderness and Spotsylvania were defeats.

During the fighting on 9 May, Sedgwick, commander of Union VI Corps, was riding up and down his front lines, exhorting his men. He told them: 'The Confederates could not hit an elephant at this distance.' Seconds later a Confederate sharpshooter shot him dead.

Cold Harbor (Second Cold Harbor), Virginia, 31 May to 12 June 1864

Grant's Overland Campaign, May–June 1864

Union:
Lieutenant-General Ulysses S. Grant
Army of the Potomac
*c.*103,875 men
(total casualties 12,737)

Confederate:
General Robert E. Lee
Army of Northern Virginia
*c.*64,000 men
(total casualties 2,500)

On the afternoon of 31 May Sheridan's Union cavalry seized the vital crossroads known as Old Cold Harbor, holding it until the lead elements of the Army of the Potomac supported him.

Reinforcements did not arrive until about 09.00 the following day. Significant numbers of Confederate infantry were contesting the area. Union VI and XVIII Corps reached Cold Harbor later in the afternoon and drove the Confederates back, taking several hundred prisoners.

By 2 June both the Union and Confederate armies had deployed on a seven-mile front, extending from the Chickahominy River all the way to Bethesda Church. Grant was busy organising a major offensive to take place that afternoon, but Union troops were not quite in place, so the assault was postponed until 04.30 on 3 June. It was to be led by Union II and XVIII Corps and supported by IX Corps. No sooner had the advance got under way than the air was filled with artillery shells and musket balls. All along the Bethesda Church to Cold Harbor line Union troops were being slaughtered. They marched forward for around eight minutes amidst the withering fire. In the few places where Union troops reached the Confederate positions they had some success and captured several hundred prisoners, but gradually the assault was being pinned down and in places troops withdrew.

Grant was adamant that a co-ordinated assault should have carried the Confederate line, but rather than moving towards the flank of the enemy, the Union corps had hit it straight on. Shortly after mid-day the Union troops withdrew in places, but dug in on positions which they had captured. The battlefield was strewn with wounded and dead and in the summer heat there was very bad suffering. It was not until the third day after the assault on 3 June that many of the wounded were recovered, by which time it was too late for a significant number of them.

The two armies sat and stared at one another until 12 June. By this time both armies had considerably improved their entrenchments, and zigzagged trench lines scarred the battlefield. Nearly every morning at 09.00 throughout the wait the Confederates had opened fire with their artillery and muskets all along

the front, in the hope that the Union troops had withdrawn during the night.

On 12 June Grant decided that nothing more could be achieved, and determined to cross the James River and threaten Petersburg. Accordingly, on 14 June II Corps was ferried across the river at Wilcox's Landing, and on the 15th the rest of the army was withdrawn across the James River via a 2,200 ft pontoon bridge which had been thrown up at Weyanoke. Grant realised that he could not break through this portion of the defence line constructed around Richmond.

All in all, Cold Harbor was a very discouraging battle, fought on nearly the same ground as Gaines's Mill two years before. Grant was later to say in his memoirs:

'Cold Harbor is, I think, the only battle I ever fought that I would not fight over again under any circumstances. I have always regretted that the last assault of Cold Harbor was ever made.'

While Grant's troops were being held at Cold Harbor, Sheridan's cavalry had cut loose, and with around 8,000 men, left New Castle on 7 June and reached Buck Child's, three miles from Trevilian Station, on the 10th. He intended to cut the main railroad line at the station. He was closely pursued by Hampton and Fitzhugh Lee, but by 11 June Sheridan was ready to strike. He drove the Confederates back towards the station, finally routing them in the direction of Gordonsville and Louisa Court House.

Amongst Sheridan's commanders was General Custer, leading his Michigan cavalry. After capturing the station Sheridan discovered that Breckinridge's infantry had reached Lynchburg, so during the night of the 12th Sheridan recrossed the North Anna at Carpenter's Ford with a large quantity of supplies and hundreds of prisoners that he had captured during his ride.

On 18 June Sheridan received orders to proceed to the supply depot at White House, where he was to bring its contents towards Petersburg and reunite with Grant's troops. Accordingly he crossed the Mattapony River and by the 24th was under way to Petersburg with 900 wagons. He was attacked at St Mary's Church by Hampton's cavalry; but leaving his sub-commander Gregg to hold off the Confederates, he managed to slip through, and by 29 June had crossed over the James River at Wilcox's Landing.

From 5 May to 1 August 1864 Sheridan's cavalry corps had lost around 5,500 men. They had captured 2,000 Confederates, huge quantities of supplies and horses, and, what is more, Sheridan had engaged large numbers of Confederates in the fruitless task of pursuing him across the countryside.

Cold Harbor battle line. (Malcolm Waddy III)

Grant's tactics at Cold Harbor and at Spotsylvania have been severely criticised for the wastefulness of men. Grant described his tactics in battle by the single phrase 'hammer continuously'. The result was that Grant was losing twenty men to every one that Lee lost. By this stage of the war there was no doubt that the Confederacy was exhausted, but such an unequal loss of men could not be sustained for an indefinite period. In comparison to the Atlanta Campaign that had been led by Sherman in very similar circumstances, the tactics of Grant were brutal to say the least. Each time Sherman had come up against determined Confederate positions, he had been willing to entrench himself around them and then strangle the enemy out of the fortifications by cutting off supplies and communication. Whether Grant was looking for a faster resolution to the conflict so late in the war is unknown, but he was perfectly prepared to dash his troops against the rocks of Confederate fortifications, whatever the cost.

Confederate General Johnston, writing of the beginning of the campaign that pitted him against Sherman in the struggle for possession of Atlanta, summed up the point by commenting: 'I know I should have beaten him, had he made such assaults on me as General Grant did on Lee.'

Despite this, the end of the Confederate States of America was less than a year away.

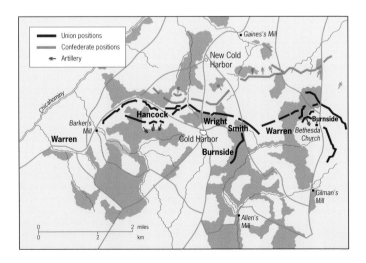

Opequon (Third Winchester), Virginia, 19 September 1864

Sheridan's Shenandoah Valley Campaign, August–December 1864

Union:
Major-General Philip Sheridan
c.39,240 men
(total casualties 5,020)

Confederate:
Lieutenant-General Jubal A. Early
c.15,200 men
(total casualties 3,610)

Opequon was the largest and most important battle fought in the Shenandoah. The battle was a turning point from which the Union cause continued to rise as the Confederate decline hastened.

Grant sent Sheridan into the valley to deal with the Confederates once and for all. On 19 September at 02.00 Sheridan's army left Berryville, and by dawn lead elements were crossing the Opequon near Spout Spring. From here they entered the Berryville Canyon which was contested by Confederates under Ramseur. He held the cavalry until he was reinforced. As the Union cavalry withdrew, Sheridan's infantry deployed. Meanwhile Sheridan had ordered Merrit's cavalry towards the Seiver's and Locke's fords. Here they were opposed by Confederate cavalry under McCausland. He held until 10.30, then withdrew. The Union cavalry advanced, encountering Confederate infantry at 11.00. The latter withdrew at noon to rejoin the main Confederate army facing Sheridan's infantry.

Back at the canyon, the Union XIX Corps advanced on the right and was slaughtered by Confederate artillery and ferocious counter-attacks. On the left the Union VI Corps smashed into Ramseur and pushed him back as far as Dinkle's Barn. However, Rodes's Confederates counter-attacked, taking advantage of the gap between the Union XIX and VI Corps.

It seemed that Sheridan was beaten, but he threw in his reserves and pushed the Confederates back into the West Woods.

By now, Union cavalry was engaged on the Valley Pike, and at 10.00 Merrit had reached Stephenson's Depot. He was reinforced here by Averell and Devin. McCausland retreated to entrenchments near Collier Redoubt.

Sheridan now ordered up Crook's troops at 13.00. Some were sent to aid the XIX Corps in First Woods. Crucially an eighteen-gun battery under DuPont accompanied this move and turned the Confederate flank with its fire. The Confederates now retreated to the Second Woods.

By 15.30 Union cavalry had carried McCausland's positions, and all along the Confederate front Sheridan was pressing forward. Early's army was in grave danger of being surrounded and overrun. His troops only just managed to extricate themselves through the prompt rearguard action of General Rodes. In disorder, Early fell back on Kernstown and then onto Fisher's Hill.

Fisher's Hill, Virginia, 21–22 September 1864

Sheridan's Shenandoah Campaign, August–September 1864

Union:
Major-General Philip Sheridan
29,444 men
(total casualties 528)

Confederate:
Lieutenant-General Jubal A. Early
9,500 men
(total casualties 1,235)

Smarting from the defeat at Opequon (Third Battle of Winchester) on 19 September, Early's Confederates set up camp on Fisher's Hill. Defensively, this was a good position, occupying a dominant feature south of Strasburg.

Early's headquarters was located in a house on Valley Pike, his artillery covered all approaches to the deployment area and signal stations had been established to give him early warning of a Union advance.

Sheridan's army left the Strasburg area at noon on 21 September, advancing south and west. The bulk of the army moved to a plateau north of Flint Hill and began to entrench. Flint Hill was one of a line of hills to the north of Tumbling Run held by Confederate skirmishers in advance of Early's main lines. After several attempts, Sheridan's men drove the Confederates off the hills, and by nightfall were digging in within musket range of the Confederates. During the night Sheridan extended his front line west, and at sunrise the whole Union army advanced, first taking Quarry Hill. An artillery duel developed along the battle front as Sheridan sent General Crook to find the Confederate left flank. It was held by Lomax's cavalry and they were quickly dispersed. Crook continued to advance, but was checked by Confederates at Ramseur's Hill.

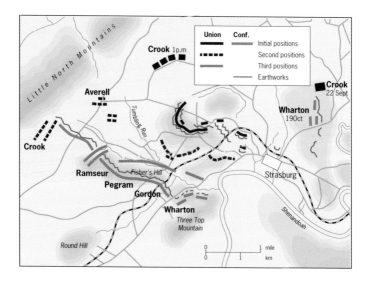

Pressure on the Confederate left was building, added to which there was fighting all along the main battle line. Gradually the Confederates, desperate not to be flanked by Sheridan, began to fall back to the rear. Soon Early's army was in a shambles, but an attempt to regain control was successful on Round Hill, and a rearguard was established on Prospect Hill by Generals Ramseur, Gordon and Pegram. The Confederates retreated through the Narrow Passage (Rockfish Gap, near Waynesboro), having been saved by Confederate cavalry in the Lurany Valley from the threat of being surrounded.

The road was now clear, and Sheridan advanced to Staunton. In October, he withdrew from the valley, but not before laying its farms to waste. The valley, so long the bread-basket of Lee's army, could barely feed itself. Sheridan's 'scorched earth' policy in the valley has become known as the 'Burning', or 'Red October'.

Chaffin's Farm (New Market Heights), Virginia, 29–30 September 1864
Richmond–Petersburg Campaign, June 1864 to March 1865

Union:
Major-General Benjamin Butler

Confederate:
General Robert E. Lee
Lieutenant-General Richard S. Ewell

(total casualties 4,430)

On the night of 28 September, Union General Grant sent Major-General Benjamin Butler's Army of the James across the James River to attack Confederate defence works north of the river. This was Lee's left flank defending Richmond.

Butler's troops marched for twelve hours from their positions at Petersburg, seventeen miles north-east. At dawn, they found themselves facing elements of Hood's Texas Brigade holding New Market Heights.

Significantly, Butler had chosen Brigadier-General Paine's 3rd Division of XVIII Corps, which were United States Colored Troops (USCT). Their objective, the Confederate earthworks, lay some 300 yards away, bisected by a stream, marshland, abatis and sharpened stakes.

The assault began at 05.30 in clearing fog, Duncan's brigade leading. Duncan's men suffered over 50 per cent casualties, but a second assault went in at 06.00, this time getting to within thirty yards of the Texans.

Meanwhile Fort Harrison, a key defensive position in the Confederate line, was under threat. The Texans holding the defence works against the USCT were ordered to reinforce the fort. Under cover of Virginian cavalry, the Texans withdrew and the USCT swarmed over the Confederate positions; by 07.00 New Market Heights was in Union hands.

The fighting around New Market Heights had claimed 54 per cent of all the USCT engaged, despite the fact that they only accounted for 20 per cent of Butler's men.

42

Grant's plan, however, had worked. Lee was moving troops from Petersburg to protect Richmond. After the fall of Fort Harrison and New Market Heights, Lee managed to contain the Union breakthroughs and re-establish a line north of the James River. He counter-attacked on 30 September, cutting off the captured positions.

Despite their many detractors, the USCT had acquitted themselves well in the battle. During the engagement, regardless of casualties, which had claimed most of their officers, the USCT did not waver. Some sixteen Medals of Honor were presented to African Americans during the American Civil War, fourteen of them for their bravery on New Market Heights.

Union cavalry charge. (American Civil War Society)

Saltville, Virginia, 2 October 1864 and 20–21 December 1864

Burbridge's Raid into South-west Virginia, September–October 1864 and Stoneman's Raid into South-west Virginia, December 1864

2 October 1864
Union:
Brigadier-General Stephen Burbridge
c.5,000 men

Confederate:
Brigadier-General Alfred E. Jackson
c.2,800 men

(total casualties 458)

20–21 December 1864
Union:
Major-General George Stoneman
A.C. Gillem's Division

Confederate:
Major-General John C. Breckinridge
c.1,000–1,500 men

(total casualties unknown)

In the fall of 1864, General Ulysses S. Grant gave Burbridge permission to execute a raid into south-west Virginia. His main target was the Confederate salt works at Saltville. Significantly some 600 of his men were the V US Colored Cavalry (USCC). Burbridge's march was delayed *en route* by around 300 Confederates under Giltner at Clinch Mountain

and Laurel Gap, which allowed Jackson to concentrate troops at Saltville.

The Union troops were within two miles of Saltville by the evening of 1 October. The Confederates held the high ground in front of Saltville. Burbridge's men managed to push the Confederates off Sander's Hill, and at around 10.00 on the 2nd began a series of attacks on Chestnut Ridge. After two unsuccessful attempts Burbridge threw in the V USCC, the XII Ohio and the XI Michigan. The V Corps managed to breach the Confederate defences, but after six hours of heavy fighting, Union ammunition was running short. Burbridge was forced to fall back, particularly given the fact that Breckinridge's cavalry had arrived to reinforce the Confederates.

What is particularly significant is the aftermath of the battle, when it is said that Tennessee troops murdered prisoners and wounded of the V USCC. Estimates of between 46 and 150 have been quoted. These murders were taken seriously enough for Lee to write to Breckinridge, saying that he was:

'... much pained to hear of the treatment the Negro prisoners are reported to have received, and agrees with you entirely in condemning it. That a general officer should have been guilty of the crime you mentioned meets with his unqualified reprobation. He directs that if the officer is still in your department you prefer charges against him and bring him to trial.'

It seems that as far as Breckinridge was concerned, the fault lay with General Felix Robertson, but he had abandoned his command and joined Joe Wheeler's Confederate brigands.

Burbridge retreated after the battle, and by the next morning, 3 October, was twenty miles away. He was pursued by the Confederates as far as the head of the Louisa fork of the Big Sandy River.

In December 1864 General Stoneman was ordered to enter south-west Virginia and establish Union control of the area. He had around 4,000 cavalry with him, and Breckinridge faced him with certainly fewer

than 1,500 men. The Confederates concentrated around the salt works at Saltville, defending similar positions to those they had held in October. Stoneman, however, used his superior mobility to capture as much as he could whilst the Confederates were entrenched at Saltville. He occupied Bristol and Abingdon, bypassing Saltville and heading for Wytheville and the lead mines.

Breckinridge was forced to move, and managed to intercept Stoneman on 18 December, fighting an engagement at Marion, where his troops succeeded in beating off Stoneman's cavalry. Whilst the battle was raging, Stoneman sent troops back towards Saltville, and after having routed the militia which Breckinridge had left there, succeeded in capturing and destroying the salt works. His troops had melted away before Breckinridge could get back to Saltville and face the Union cavalry.

Having accomplished his objectives, Stoneman withdrew across the mountains. But he would be back. On 27 February 1865, via General Thomas, commanding officer of the Department of the Cumberland, Stoneman received orders from Grant to 'repeat the raid of last fall, destroying the railroad as far toward Lynchburg as he can'.

This time he met even less opposition, and after having left Knoxville, he rode to Morristown, Bull's Gap and then to Boone in North Carolina. From Boone he headed into south-west Virginia and destroyed the Virginia and Tennessee railroad from Wytheville to Lynchburg. By 9 April he was back in North Carolina, and after destroying the railroad between Greensboro and Danville, Virginia, he entered Salisbury on the 12th. Here he captured nearly 1,400 Confederates and fourteen artillery pieces.

Cedar Creek, Virginia, 19 October 1864
Sheridan's Shenandoah Valley Campaign, August–December 1864

Union:
Major-General Philip Sheridan
Major-General Horatio Wright*
Army of the Shenandoah
*c.*31,945 men
(total casualties 5,665)
*commanded the army during Sheridan's temporary absence early in the battle

Confederate:
Lieutenant-General Jubal Early
*c.*21,000 men
(total casualties 2,910)

At dawn on 19 October 1864, the Confederate army under Early surprised the Union troops at Cedar Creek. It was a bold move which initially routed the

Union VIII and XIX Corps, but the timely arrival of Sheridan to rally his men broke the back of the Confederates and snatched a vital victory, leading to the re-election of Abraham Lincoln.

Early had learnt that Sheridan was about to send part of his army to Grant, and consequently he marched on Fisher's Hill, arriving there on 13 October. He encamped there until the 16th, his scouts having already discovered that Sheridan's army was in force on the north bank of Cedar Creek.

The Confederates discovered that Sheridan's left flank was only lightly guarded and that the bulk of the Union cavalry was on the right flank. Early decided to send General Gordon's troops, along with those of Ramseur and Pegram, across the river and round the enemy's left flank. Early himself, supported by Kershaw, Wharton and all of the artillery, would pin down Sheridan's front and left.

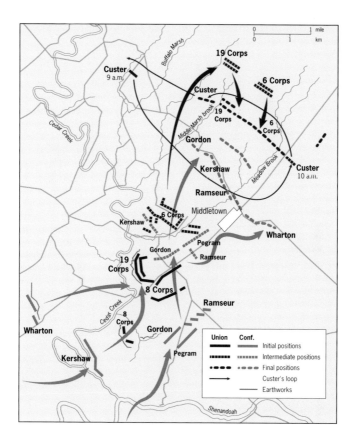

The attack was scheduled for 05.00, just before daybreak, and as soon as Gordon's men were engaged, cavalry under Rosser would attack the few Union cavalry on the left. Lomax's remaining cavalry would then cross the river and strike where needed. With the intention of catching the Union troops unawares, all of the Confederate infantry were told to leave their swords and canteens in the camp to reduce noise and avoid warning Union pickets.

At 01.00, Confederate scouts spotted the Union entrenchments on the route of Gordon's march, and by 03.30 Early was sure that he now knew the Union deployments, as he could see the campfires for himself. As the Confederates moved forward in the moonlight, skirmishers opened fire at around 04.30, but by 05.00 Early had directed Kershaw's men to assault the Union left, capturing seven guns. Meanwhile, Early could hear that Gordon was engaged to the rear of the Union army. Crook's Union troops on the left had been swept aside as soon as they realised that Gordon was behind them, and both the XIV and Crook's troops were in full retreat.

On the right Pegram had run into VI Corps. Early supported him with Wharton's troops, but because of the fog, the Confederate attack was uncoordinated and was thrown back. Union cavalry was advancing to the right of Middletown, threatening the Confederates' own right and rear. This move was beaten off by Early positioning some twenty guns. The fog was still causing problems for both armies: not only were they unsure where the enemy were concentrating, but they did not know where their fellow formations were located.

Still the Confederate flank was exposed, particularly at Middletown. Union cavalry were making strong attempts, but the timely arrival of Lomax eased the situation. Rosser faced considerable opposition from the Union mounted troops. The bulk of the Union army had taken up new positions some two miles north of Middletown.

Early desperately wanted to push on and force the enemy from their new positions; equally, an attack now would deny the routed Union troops an opportunity to re-form. Nevertheless, he was forced to accept that this would not be possible. Firstly, enemy cavalry still threatened his left flank; secondly, a good number of Confederates were looting the abandoned Union camps, and finally, marching over the difficult terrain during the night had disordered and scattered many of his men.

The unavoidable delays allowed the Union cavalry to regain some semblance of order. Early took the opportunity to collect abandoned weapons and wagons, whilst his men held off increasingly determined Union cavalry attacks.

By late afternoon, the Union army had rallied sufficiently, particularly following the arrival of their commander, who had been in Winchester. Sheridan seemed to galvanise the army, and although Early thought the day was won, the Union commander clearly thought otherwise.

Sheridan's infantry advanced against the whole of the Confederate front, puncturing it on the left. Evans's brigade gave way, followed by Gordon's other troops. Now Early faced the very real prospect of losing everything, but he successfully held off renewed Union cavalry charges. Kershaw's and Ramseur's men joined in the retreat, and nothing, it would seem, could stop them.

Ramseur himself, with just two brigades and artillery, held off Sheridan long enough for Early's army to retire. Ramseur was mortally wounded in his ninety-minute stand. Attempts to rally the Confederate troops at Cedar Creek failed, which led to the grievous loss of the bulk of Early's ammunition and supply wagons. Sheridan's troops, now in command of the battle, were content with a gradual advance. Significantly, a bridge on the narrow road between Strasburg and Fisher's Hill collapsed, stranding most of Early's remaining supplies, which were captured by Union cavalry.

The bulk of the Confederate infantry halted at Fisher's Hill and at 03.00 on 20 October, Rosser covered the retreat to New Market. He remained in place until around 10.00, not ever being threatened by Sheridan.

Sheridan's return from Winchester had turned the battle. Early was very close to rolling up the entire Union army. Sheridan's ability to regroup a beaten army, counter-attack and drive Early's men from the field won him justifiable praise. The Union general's prompt action is immortalised in Thomas Buchanan Read's classic poem *Sheridan's Ride*.

As far as the Confederates were concerned, a glorious victory had been snatched away from them. Certainly, the fact that so many of the Confederates were busy looting at the crucial time when Early could have finished off the enemy is a critical consideration, as is the fact that suddenly the Confederates, so solid and determined, chose to retire despite the pleas of their commanders.

In part, regardless of the defeat, Early had stopped Sheridan from sending men to Grant, further threatening the position of General Lee.

By 9 November Sheridan was established at Kernstown. Most of Early's army was recalled to Richmond in early December, leaving Early with just Wharton's division and some artillery and cavalry stationed at Staunton.

Appomattox, Virginia, 25 March to 9 April 1865
Appomattox Campaign, March–April 1865

Union:
Lieutenant-General Ulysses S. Grant
Army of the Potomac
Army of the Shenandoah
Army of the James
c.120,000 men
(total casualties 10,515 men)

Confederate:
General Robert E. Lee
5 corps
c.54,000 men
(28,356 surrendered, some 19,132 had already been captured)

As the spring of 1865 approached, Lee's Confederates, numbering fewer than 50,000, faced the juggernaut that was Grant's vast Union army of 112,000. Grant's plans were clear: continue to pressurise Lee at Petersburg, cut him off from his supplies and force a surrender. As for Lee, he planned to break out of the siege lines and launch another great assault on the North. Perhaps if Lee could break out and join with Johnson, then they could defeat Sherman in North Carolina and turn on Grant himself. It was an all-risk strategy.

Accordingly, Lee sent Gordon off to draw Grant away, which would mean that he could slip south to join Johnston. Gordon failed and the Confederacy lost 5,000 much-needed men. The move also alerted Grant to Lee's plan; they both knew that the South Side Railway was the only route left to the Confederates if they wanted to get to North Carolina.

On 29 March Grant sent Sheridan to Five Forks and Lee sent his nephew Fitzhugh Lee there, although Pickett would have overall command of the Confederates. Ultimately it was too much to ask 10,000 Confederates to outmanoeuvre and beat 28,000 Union troops. Sheridan captured Five Forks, the South Side Railway and 4,000 prisoners.

Lee now knew that he must abandon Petersburg, but he realised that this would not be an easy operation. In any case, if Lee had thought that Grant would just stand by and let him fall back, then he was wrong.

On 2 April, before dawn, Union troops advanced on all fronts, emerging through thick fog. By noon, Lee's western line had been shattered, except for a stout defence of Fort Gregg. A.P. Hill was killed in an encounter with Union infantry, and Gordon was just holding Petersburg against the Union IV Corps. By 20.00 the Confederates were in full retreat, and their artillery had to be spiked and abandoned. In the early hours of 3 April, Richmond was abandoned, soon to fall into Union hands. Lee's commanders were all heading towards the Appomattox; the roads were clogged with troops, all organisation gone.

Remarkably, Lee's five different commands that had been spread out over forty miles on 2 April came together at Amelia Court House two days later. Grant, meanwhile, had sent Sheridan west towards Jetersville, ten miles south-west of the Amelia Court House. He figured that by cutting off Lee's last hope of reaching Johnston, he would force his old

Appomattox Court House. (US National Archive)

adversary to surrender. Once Grant had taken Petersburg, he despatched infantry to support Sheridan, hoping that whichever way Lee turned, he would find Union troops.

On 4 April, 30,000 Confederate soldiers had been concentrated at Amelia Court House. Lee was determined to fight on, but wished to avoid Grant's advancing infantry. Supplies, and particularly food, were short but the Confederates foraged as best they could in the local area.

On the morning of 5 April Lee's men marched off towards Jetersville. Just beyond the town Sheridan had entrenched his cavalry and barred the way forward. To dally here was dangerous for the Confederates, as Union infantry were closing in. Reluctantly Lee decided to head for Farmville on the Appomattox. He hoped that supplies could reach him there from Lynchburg, which was forty miles further on.

Sunrise on 6 April found Lee's troops at Saylor's Creek; Meade's Union infantry had reached Amelia Court House and Sheridan had been sent to Farmville. Sheridan's cavalry had been harassing the Confederates all along the route of march, but at Saylor's Creek he had an opportunity. He concentrated his cavalry and surrounded Ewell and Anderson, who were at the rear of the column. Despite an initial sharp fight, the stuffing was knocked out of the Confederates by artillery fire, and 6,000 men and nine generals fell into Union hands. Lee had lost half of his army; many more Confederates had simply given in. Longstreet made it to Farmville the next morning. Lee's remnants followed and rested, then headed west in the evening of 7 April.

Grant was close behind, reaching Farmville shortly after the Confederates had abandoned it. It was clear

that Lee was beaten, but the stubborn Confederate was heading for Appomattox Station, twenty-two miles away, to collect a train-load of supplies.

It was at Farmville that Grant sent the first letter to Lee requesting the surrender of the Army of Northern Virginia. Lee's response was, 'Not yet' and on he marched into the morning of the 8th.

By nightfall, Lee was two miles from Appomattox Court House, and Appomattox Station and the supplies were just three miles away. Lee now heard that Sheridan was heading for the station but still believed he could get there first.

That night Grant sent another letter; Lee replied that he would not discuss surrender, but would talk about a negotiated peace. Grant declined; he had no authority to do this, only to accept surrender.

Events were to overtake them both, for at 21.00 on 8 April Sheridan reached Appomattox Station first. There was no escape now. Lee was trapped and without supplies. One hope remained: if Sheridan was not there in force, Lee could yet escape.

At 05.00 on 9 April, Gordon and Fitzhugh Lee hit Sheridan's lines; there was no support as Longstreet was holding back Meade and Humphreys to the rear. Sheridan had been reinforced; the game was up.

At 08.30 Lee rode off hoping to meet Grant at his proposed time of 10.00. When he reached the Union lines, he was given Grant's reply declining the meeting. The old Confederate general now requested an interview to discuss the surrender of his army. It took until 12.15 for Grant to get the request.

Inside the McLean House Lee signed the surrender, and by 16.00 he was heading back to his army to tell them it was all over.

Five Forks, Virginia, 1 April 1865

Appomattox Campaign, March–April 1865

Union:
Major-General Philip Sheridan
c.26,000 men
(total casualties 830)

Confederate:
Major-General George Pickett
c.7,000 men initially engaged
(total casualties 2,950)

Following his successful Shenandoah Campaign, Sheridan was keen to begin an offensive against the Confederate lines defending Petersburg. If the South Side Railroad could be severed, then Richmond's last rail link with the south would be cut.

Robert E. Lee, the Confederate commander, was also perfectly well aware of the importance of holding this line. He had faced Grant for ten months at Petersburg, where superior Union numbers allowed Grant to extend the line westwards, stretching the thin Confederate defences to breaking point. Grant recognised that the key position was Five Forks, south-west of Petersburg, five miles from the battle line and just three from the railroad.

Accordingly, on 29 March, Lee ordered General George E. Pickett's 14,000 troops, supported by 5,000 cavalry, to Five Forks. Meanwhile, Union pressure around the Confederate right was building. By

31 March, Sheridan was pinning down the bulk of the Confederates in the area when he sent Major-General Warren's troops onto the Confederate left. Initially, he overwhelmed the Confederates, taking a great number of men captive.

As Warren approached Five Forks, on 1 April, Pickett counter-attacked, forcing him back to Dinwiddie Court House. Five Forks and the railroad had been held, but Lee had already told Jefferson Davis, the Confederate president, that in his opinion he must soon evacuate Petersburg and Richmond.

When Pickett informed Lee of his victory, he was told 'Hold Five Forks at all hazards!' As for Warren, he had failed, and Sheridan relieved him of his command of V Corps.

Pickett's message to Lee was premature, for at 16.00 Sheridan ordered a general assault which drove the Confederates back some miles. Confederates everywhere were being overrun and surrendering in increasing numbers. A new assault was timed for 04.00 the following day, and the intensity of the attack was so great, and the confusion of the Confederates so complete, that Petersburg surrendered at 04.28 to Union forces. General Grant, overall commander of the campaign, rode triumphantly into the city at 09.00. It was indeed the greatest disaster suffered by the Army of Northern Virginia. For many, it has been henceforth called the 'Confederate Waterloo'.

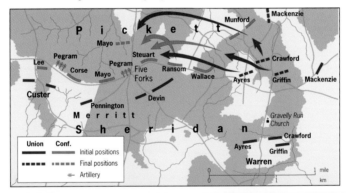

The Battle at Five Forks. (Library of Congress)

Union:
Lieutenant-General Ulysses S. Grant
c.120,000 men
(total casualties 3,500)

Confederate:
General Robert E. Lee
c.54,000 men
(total casualties 4,250)

Following the Confederate defeat at Five Forks on 1 April, Grant's army prepared itself for a major offensive against the Petersburg defences. The assault would be a combined attack by Humphreys's II Corps, Wright's VI Corps, Parke's IX Corps and Gibbon's XXIV Corps. The assault was delayed in clearing the field of abandoned defence works which would have disorganised the troops.

As dawn rose, the attack began at 04.45, preceded by an enormous artillery bombardment. By 05.15 Wright had carried his portion of the line, and shortly afterwards Parke, too, had penetrated the Confederate defences. Sheridan, meanwhile, along with Warren's V Corps, had swung round from the west and the Confederates were in grave danger of being completely cut off. At 07.30 Humphreys broke through, and Confederate prisoners were beginning to flood back through the defence works.

Lee was desperately trying to hold back Parke's Corps, which was threatening his inner line and the bridge across the Appomattox. He was being reinforced by Longstreet and made some progress.

By noon the whole of the outer Confederate defence works were in Union hands, with the exception of Forts Gregg and Whitworth. Three Union brigades attempted to dislodge the three-hundred-man garrison in Fort Gregg, led by Lieutenant-Colonel Duncan, and from 13.00 to 14.30 they held out against overwhelming odds, until they finally surrendered. Fort Whitworth was abandoned, and the sixty men who had held the fort surrendered.

Meanwhile Union troops had struck at Sutherland's Station, capturing 1,000 Confederates. Grant was so sure now of a victory that he sent Abraham Lincoln a telegram at 16.40, inviting him to pay a visit to Petersburg the following day. The inner lines of the Confederate defences still held, but Grant was certain that Lee would evacuate Petersburg that night.

Lee began his withdrawal at 22.00 and it was completed before 03.00 on 3 April. At 09.00 that day Union troops marched into Petersburg.

Abraham Lincoln met Grant in the city of Petersburg, and he was showing obvious signs of delight that the struggle was nearly over. At 12.30 Grant sent another telegram, this one to Major-General Weitzel, who had been moving on Richmond, and then rode off towards Sutherland's Station before

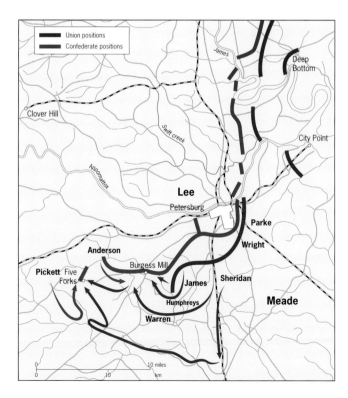

he received Weitzel's reply. It read: 'We took Rich-mond at 8:15 this morning. I captured many guns. Enemy left in great haste. The city is on fire in two places. Am making every effort to put it out.'

By 03.00 on the 4th, Grant and the Army of the Potomac were on the move again, with Sheridan in the lead. Orde's Army of the James was heading towards Burkeville to head off Lee from Danville, where Lee hoped to join Johnston's army. By the evening Grant was 27 miles west of Petersburg, and by noon on the 5th the army had reached a point 10 miles east of Burkeville, at Nottoway Court House. It was here that Grant received the news that Sheridan had intercepted Lee and that the Confederate army was at Amelia Court House.

The Union forces were quickly converging on Lee, and on the night of the 6th the Confederates retreated towards Farmville. By noon on the 7th Grant himself was at Farmville, where he began the correspondence with Lee that would lead to the surrender of the Army of Northern Virginia.

Weitzel's men had not had to fight for the posses-sion of the Confederate capital. At first light on 3 April his army had approached the city, preceded by forty men acting as scouts. His aide-de-camp, Graves, wrote:

'As we approached the inner line of the defences we saw in the distance divisions of our troops, many of them upon the double-quick, aiming to be the first in the city; a white and a colored division were having a regular race, the white troops on the turnpike and the colored in the fields. As we neared the city the fires seemed to increase in number and size, and at intervals loud explo-sions were heard. There was absolutely no plundering upon the part of our soldiers; orders were issued forbidding anything to be taken without remuneration, and no com-plaints were made of infringement of these orders.'

Western Theatre

Mill Springs (Logan's Crossroads, Fishing Creek), Kentucky, 19 January 1862
Offensive in Eastern Kentucky, 1862

Union:
Brigadier-General George H. Thomas
1st Division, Army of the Ohio
Brigadier-General A. Schoepf's Brigade
(total casualties 232)

Confederate:
Major-General George B. Crittenden
2 brigades
(total casualties 439)

Brigadier-General Felix K. Zollicoffer advanced from the Cumberland Gap in November 1861 into Kentucky and dug in around Mill Springs for the winter. He was careful to fortify the area, particular-ly both sides of the Cumberland River.

Meanwhile, Brigadier-General Thomas had received orders to attack Crittenden's army and push the Confederates across the Cumberland River. The weather was extremely poor and conditions meant that it took him a considerable time to reach Logan's Crossroads. He was due to meet Brigadier-General Schoepf's men, who were marching from Somerset. He, himself, had come from Lebanon.

Crittenden was aware of the Union movements and consequently rode to Mill Springs and took personal command of the Confederate troops. Rather than wait for Thomas to deploy and choose where he wished to attack, Crittenden decided to go on the offensive himself. They encountered Thomas's pick-et line at Logan's Crossroads at about 06.30 on 19 January. Crittenden was unaware of the fact that Schoepf's troops had arrived, but the Confederate attack proceeded well until Union resistance stiffened along a fence line and ridge near the crossroads.

Bizarrely, Colonel Speed S. Fry and General Zollicoffer both rode forward amidst the smoke and dense woodland to find out what was going on. Fry mistook Zollicoffer for a Union officer and apologised for having ordered his men to fire at Zollicoffer's men. Suddenly one of Zollicoffer's staff rode up to warn the general that he was talking to a Union officer, and fired his pistol at Fry. Fry and the Union soldiers near him returned fire and Zollicoffer fell dead to the ground. Amidst the confusion Union troops counter-attacked the Confederate right and left, and the Confederates began to retire from the field.

At least in part the Confederate failure was a result of their attempts to use obsolete flintlock muskets in the poor weather conditions. One account suggests that only one in five of the Confederate muskets would fire.

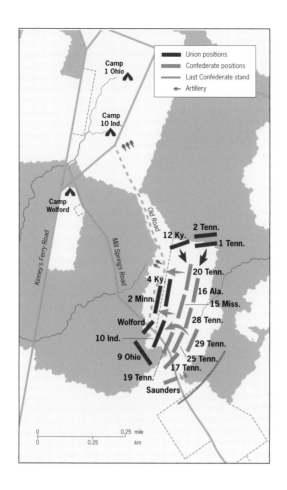

Union positions
Confederate positions
Last Confederate stand
Artillery

Camp
1 Ohio

Camp
10 Ind.

Camp
Wolford

Old Road

Kinney's Ferry Road

Mill Springs Road

12 Ky. 2 Tenn.
        1 Tenn.

20 Tenn.

4 Ky. 16 Ala.

2 Minn. 15 Miss.

Wolford 28 Tenn.

10 Ind. 29 Tenn.

9 Ohio 25 Tenn.

17 Tenn.

19 Tenn.

Saunders

0   0.25 mile
0   0.25   km

The Battle of Mill Springs. (Library of Congress)

Union:
Brigadier-General Ulysses S. Grant
3 infantry divisions
c.15,000 men
6 ironclads and gunboats
(total casualties 2,331–2,886)

Confederate:
Brigadier-General Gideon J. Pillow
Brigadier-General John B. Floyd
Brigadier-General Simon B. Buckner
Fort Donelson garrison
Strength unclear
(total casualties, including 12,000 captured, *c*.15,067)

After Union General Grant captured Fort Henry on 6 February, he advanced on Fort Donelson with the intention of cutting Texas off from the rest of the Southern states. The capture of the two forts would also help to isolate Tennessee. Fort Donelson was some eleven miles from Fort Henry, and using similar tactics which involved blockading the fort by river with ironclads and gunboats, Grant sought to strangle the garrison.

Grant's investment of Fort Donelson was completed on the afternoon of 12 February. Vigorous assaults on the 13th were thrown back with heavy losses, and Grant realised that he could accomplish little with his army alone.

Under the command of Flag Officer A.H. Foote on the 14th, the gunboats traded shots with the garrison's artillery. The *Louisville, Pittsburg, Carondelet* and the *St Louis* were all badly damaged. The boats only managed to inflict a few casualties on the Confederate batteries.

Confederate counter-attacks on the 15th were driven back, despite the fact that Buckner had deployed two-thirds of his men. From dawn to 13.00 it seemed that the Confederates might break the siege, but after seven hours they were exhausted.

By the last day of the siege Grant had been substantially reinforced and was advancing against the right wing of the Confederate defences. Despite intense Confederate opposition, Buckner finally asked for terms, to which Grant replied: 'No terms except unconditional and immediate surrender can be accepted, I propose to move immediately upon your works.' Buckner surrendered his garrison and Grant was renamed 'Unconditional Surrender U.S. Grant'.

There is considerable dispute as to the number of troops engaged at Fort Donelson. Buckner certainly believed that Grant's force exceeded 50,000 men. However, it is more likely that by the last day his troops numbered 35,000 excluding the naval contingent. Grant admits to 27,000 men on the last day. As for Confederate figures, Buckner estimated a garrison of between 12,000 and 15,000, but claimed in his official report that his garrison did not exceed 12,000 and only 9,000 surrendered to Grant.

The Battle of Fort Donelson. (Library of Congress)

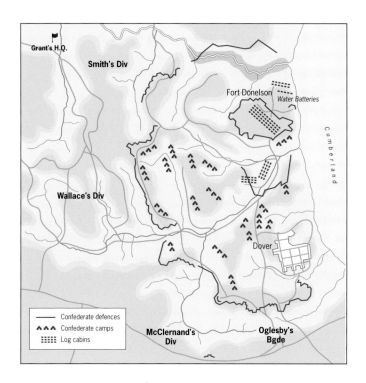

Grant's H.Q.

Smith's Div

Fort Donelson
Water Batteries

Cumberland

Wallace's Div

Dover

—— Confederate defences
∧∧∧ Confederate camps
▦▦▦ Log cabins

McClernand's
Div

Oglesby's
Bgde

Shiloh (Pittsburg Landing), Tennessee, 6–7 April 1862
Union Campaign on the Cumberland and Tennessee Rivers, 1862

Union:
Major-General Ulysses S. Grant
Army of the Tennessee
Major-General Don Carlos Buell
Army of the Ohio
c.66,812 men
170 artillery pieces
(total casualties 13,047: 1,754 killed, 8,408
wounded, 2,885 captured or missing)

Confederate:
General Albert Sidney Johnston
Army of the Mississippi I Corps
Major-General Leonidas Polk
Army of the Mississippi II Corps
Major-General Braxton Bragg
Army of the Mississippi III Corps
Major-General William J. Hardee
Army of the Mississippi Reserve Corps
Brigadier-General John C. Breckinridge
c.40,335 men
108 artillery pieces
(total casualties 10,699: 1,728 killed, 8,012
wounded, 959 captured or missing)

The winter of 1861–62 had seen Union forces
advance south from St Louis to capture the
Confederate forts of Henry and Donelson, which
commanded the Tennessee and Cumberland Rivers.
The Confederates had been forced to abandon vast
areas of Kentucky and Tennessee. Johnston's
Confederates had massed at Corinth, Mississippi; his
plan was to attack Grant's army at Pittsburg Landing
before it could be reinforced by Buell's Army of the
Ohio. The Confederates set out on 2 April; Grant was
completely unaware of the impending danger.

By the night of 5 April, Johnston was in position.
Although Union patrols found the Confederates just
before dawn, the assault hit Grant at 06.30. The first
assault overran Union camps, but Sherman's division
counter-attacked until he was forced back at around
10.00–11.30.

Fighting around an area that was named the
'Hornets' Nest' had begun at 09.30, and did not stop
until 16.30 that day. Bragg's Confederates launched
twelve attacks, but still the Union troops held on.
Nearby, the Peach Orchard, now held by Prentiss's
men who had been overwhelmed in their camps in
the first assault, became the focus of Confederate
attention. If Johnston could buckle the Union line
here, then he could annihilate Grant.

53

The Battle of Shiloh. (Library of Congress)

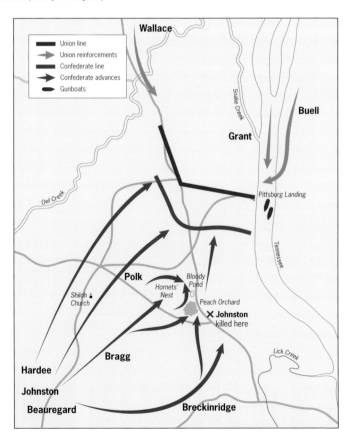

At around 14.30, in the midst of directing seven assaults against the Peach Orchard, Johnston was hit by a stray bullet which severed an artery in his leg. Johnston's death meant that Beauregard took command and established his headquarters at the recently captured Shiloh Church. At 15.30 Bragg had brought up 62 artillery pieces to pound the Hornets' Nest; under this fire Confederate infantry gained a foothold in the rear of the positions. Hurlbut's Union soldiers in the Hornets' Nest had held well, but when Union troops on his left fled, he was forced to abandon his position. Equally, the Union defence of the Peach Orchard was over. The Confederates surged forward, catching Prentiss in the rear and forcing the surrender of his 2,200 men.

Grant now had the landing with a thin crust of defenders; it was already coming under increasing pressure. In the nick of time Grant was reinforced by Ammen's Brigade and coursed by the fire from Union gunboats. The Confederates were running out of ammunition and could make no further headway; Beauregard ordered his troops to retire and reorganise.

During the evening and through the night Buell's men crossed the Tennessee River, and by morning Union troops at the landing outnumbered the Confederates.

Grant launched a counter-attack at dawn; the Confederates were exhausted, having been under continual fire from the Union gunboats all night.

Nevertheless they bitterly contested every inch that they had won the previous day, until at 14.30 they had been forced back to Shiloh Church.

Having been battered this far, Beauregard saw no advantage in contesting the field any longer. He ordered a retreat. Grant chose not to pursue too closely because, as Sherman put it: 'We had quite enough of their society for 2 whole days and were only too glad to be rid of them on any terms.'

'Bloody Shiloh' was over, the largest battle in the west of the country during the war. Most of the troops, Union and Confederate alike, had never tasted battle before. Indeed this was a terrible baptism of fire. Around a quarter of all of those engaged over the two days had become casualties.

Technically Shiloh was a draw, but strategically it was a Union triumph. The Confederacy had lost its only chance to gain the advantage in the west. Soon it would be forced to all but abandon Mississippi. Chattanooga, Corinth and Memphis would follow, and only Vicksburg would remain in Confederate hands.

Tragically, Johnston need not have died here. The shot hit him in the back of the leg and he bled to death. Had a tourniquet been applied, then it is likely that he would have survived. As was very often the case, Johnston had sent off his surgeon to help deal with Union wounded.

Memphis, Tennessee, 6 June 1862
Joint Operations on the Middle Mississippi River, 1862

Union:
Flag Officer Charles H. Davis
Colonel Charles Ellet
US ironclads *Benton, Louisville, Carondelet, Cairo, St Louis*
US Army rams *Queen of the West, Monarch*
(total casualties 1)

Confederate:
Captain James E. Montgomery
Brigadier-General M. Jeff Thompson
CS Navy rams *General Beauregard, General Bragg, General Price, General Van Dorn, General Thompson, Colonel Lovell, Sumter, Little Rebel*
(total casualties 180)

In the spring of 1862 the Union continued to focus on Tennessee as the means by which it could control the Mississippi River. Initially operations were combined arms, with Pope's infantry and Foote's gunboats detailed to tackle Confederate strongholds on the Mississippi River.

The Confederate River Defence Fleet beat the Union ironclads at Plum Run Bend, Tennessee, on 10 May, but the Federal Mississippi River Fleet was reinforced and the Confederates abandoned Fort Pil-

low and Memphis on 4 June, after the Union troops captured Corinth, Mississippi.

The Confederate naval forces were operating from Island No. 45, north of Memphis, and at 04.00 on 6 June they launched a counter-offensive against the Union fleet. They arrived off Memphis at 05.30. The battle raged for an hour and a half and proved to be disastrous for the Confederates, despite their bravery. They were hugely out-gunned and only the *General Van Dorn* escaped; all of the other Confederate vessels were either captured or sunk.

The city's leaders were quick to act as they saw the outcome of the battle, and raised the Union flag over the Court House in order to avoid the city suffering Union bombardment. Union troops immediately occupied the city, capturing its rail head, docks and shipyards. This was a massive blow for the Confederacy as Memphis was one of its most important economic and commercial centres on the Mississippi.

The Confederates had no hope of holding Memphis once their fleet had been destroyed as it is believed that they had only 200 local troops in the area. Nevertheless, they managed to destroy a good deal of the military supplies that could not be evacuated before abandoning the city to the Union troops.

Later in the war Memphis would become an important staging post for Union offensives in Mississippi.

Confederate re-enactors at the Battle of Richmond. (Robert M. Kleine)

Richmond, Kentucky, 29–30 August 1862
Kirby Smith's Confederate Offensive in Kentucky, 1862

Union:
Brigadier-General Mahlon D. Manson
1st & 2nd Brigades, Army of Kentucky
(total casualties 4,900)

Confederate:
Major-General Kirby Smith
Army of Kentucky
(total casualties 750)

When Major-General Kirby Smith launched his 1862 offensive into Kentucky he planned to blaze a trail straight through to the northern states. His advance was spearheaded by Brigadier-General Patrick R. Cleburne, with Colonel John S. Scott and his cavalry deployed to scout ahead.

On 29 August lead elements of Scott's Confederate cavalry were moving north from Big Hill *en route* to Richmond, Kentucky. Here they encountered Union cavalry, and both sides settled down to skirmishing along a broad front. By 12.00 Brigadier-General Manson, commanding the Union troops in the area, had moved up infantry and artillery to support his cavalry skirmishers. At the same time he directed the Union brigade to march towards Rogersville and close with what he believed to be the main Confederate concentration just short of Richmond. He encountered some opposition along the route

and skirmished with Cleburne's men just before nightfall.

Manson was now convinced that these skirmishes were just a precursor to a major Confederate offensive, and consequently he contacted his immediate superior, Major-General William Nelson, to apprise him of the situation. Nelson ordered that another Union brigade prepare itself to march to Manson's support should it become necessary.

Meanwhile Kirby Smith, correctly assessing that Manson was not at Richmond in any great force, conferred with Cleburne, who proposed to launch a fresh assault shortly after dawn. Cleburne was to be reinforced as well by Churchill's Division.

Cleburne's men began marching north through Kingston early in the morning. They pushed through a cordon of Union skirmishers and deployed near Manson's battle line centred round Zion Church. Throughout the day both sides would continue to reinforce, but the battle began with a customary artillery barrage. Cleburne attacked the Union right and broke through. Manson was forced to retreat towards Rogersville, where he tried to stand, but failed. Additional Union reinforcements under Smith and Nelson arrived and Nelson managed to hold the cemetery area near Richmond for a while. Ultimately the whole Union force was in flight, and nearly 4,000 of them were captured by Kirby Smith.

Buell's force skirmished with Confederate cavalry at Springfield Pike.

Union:
Major-General Don Carlos Buell
Army of the Ohio
c.61,000 men
(total casualties 4,211)

Confederate:
General Braxton Bragg
Army of the Mississippi
c.15,000–68,000 men (accounts vary)
(total casualties 3,196)

By the autumn of 1862 Braxton Bragg's Confederate invasion of Kentucky had reached Louisville. On 6 October he ordered his troops to fall back to Perryville to regroup, whilst, at the same time, Buell's Union armies were converging on Perryville in three directions. On 7 October lead elements of

The following day, shortly after dawn, Union troops advanced on the main Confederate positions. Just after noon on the 8th a Confederate counter-attack pushed the Union left flank aside. More Confederates were thrown in, but the Union army counter-attacked. As Buell continually reinforced he gained the upper hand, pushing the Confederates back into Perryville itself. Skirmishing continued throughout the evening, but with Union troops now threatening his left flank, Bragg was forced to with-draw his men, and he retreated back to Harrodsburg, then on through the Cumberland Gap and into east Tennessee.

From the first Confederate attack at 12.30, each side sought to find the other's flanks. When Bragg ordered Donelson to attack what he believed to be the Union left flank at 14.30, he was, in fact, assault-ing the centre of the Union line. By 15.00 Union

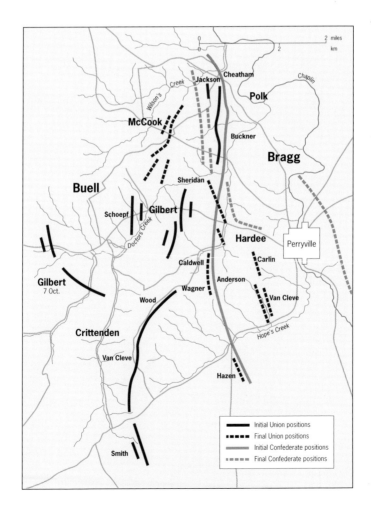

57

troops were advancing in force, but a counter-attack at 15.45 by the Confederates could have proved conclusive had Bragg been in a position to reinforce them.

Although a final Confederate advance was made at 18.30, the battle had, to all intents and purposes, been lost an hour earlier when the heights which dominated the battlefield were captured by Union troops. By this time Confederate ammunition was running desperately short, and it is to their great credit that the Confederate troops managed to hold their positions until around midnight.

Buell was unaware that the enemy had slipped away until he made a fresh advance into Perryville at 10.30 the following morning. Five hours of fighting claimed thousands of lives, with many regiments down to less than a third of their strength.

Corinth, Mississippi, 30 October 1862
Iuka and Corinth Operations, 1862

Union:
Major-General William S. Rosecrans
Army of the Mississippi
Brigadier-General Thomas A. Davies
Army of West Tennessee
c.23,000 men
(total casualties 2,520)

Confederate:
Major-General Earl Van Dorn
Army of West Tennessee
Army of the West
General Sterling Price
District of the Mississippi
Major-General Mansfield Lovell
c.22,000 men
(total casualties 4,838)

Following the Battle of Iuka (19 September), Sterling Price joined up with Earl Van Dorn's army at Ripley. As senior officer, Van Dorn took command of the combined forces. They marched to Pocahontas, reaching there on 1 October; they then headed southeast towards Corinth. Here, they encountered the defence works that Confederate troops had built the previous spring. Union forces had extended them, and within were 23,000 men.

When Van Dorn arrived at 10.00 on the 3rd, he occupied some of the outer fieldworks, then pressed forward to attack. The first Union troops were encountered beyond the defence positions; these were thrown back in short order. This retreat caused a gap between two Union brigades which Van Dorn exploited. By 13.00 Confederate troops were threatening the inner defences. As evening fell, Van Dorn was certain that he would finish off the

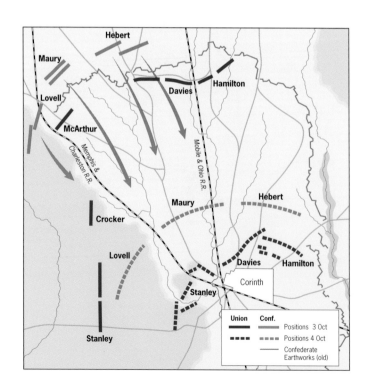

enemy in the morning and march triumphantly into Corinth.

The Confederate attack was planned to begin at daybreak, but owing to the illness of Sterling Price's 1st Division Commander, Brigadier-General Louis Hébert, it was postponed to 09.00. This gave Rosecrans vital time to reorganise, and when the Confederate assault arrived, he had placed artillery batteries in crucial positions to dominate the battlefield.

Despite mounting casualties, the Confederates stormed Battery Powell and attacked Battery Robinett, during which there was vicious hand-to-hand fighting. Some leading elements of Van Dorn's troops managed to fight their way into Corinth, but they were quickly forced back by Rosecrans. Ultimately, the Confederate attack petered out and Union troops began counter-attacking, recapturing Battery Powell. This proved to be the turning point, and Van Dorn ordered a withdrawal at 14.30. Rosecrans restored order to his army and began a pursuit the following day. He caught up with Van Dorn at Hatchie Bridge, Tennessee, on 5 October and defeated him again.

Battery Robinett is remembered as the site of some of the most desperate fighting. It was held throughout by Lieutenant Henry C. Robinett, with four Ohio regiments and the 11th Missouri. They faced the 42nd Alabama, 35th Mississippi, 2nd Texas and the 6th and 9th Texas Cavalry.

The Battle of Corinth. (Library of Congress)

Vicksburg, Mississippi, 1 May to 4 July 1863
Grant's Operations Against Vicksburg, 1863

Union:
Major-General Ulysses S. Grant
Army of the Tennessee
c.43,000 men at beginning of campaign, rising to 75,000
(total casualties 4,550 (9,362 whole campaign))

Confederate:
Lieutenant-General John C. Pemberton
c.40,000 men
(total casualties (including those who surrendered on 4 July) c.31,275)

At the same time as the Battle of Gettysburg was raging, the siege of Vicksburg was finally reaching its conclusion. Since October 1862 Grant had been trying to capture the city. In January 1863 Grant carried out a major overhaul of his army, during which he assigned McClernand to XIII Corps, Sherman to XV Corps, Hurlbut to XVI Corps and McPherson to XVII Corps. Unfortunately the majority of Hurlbut's men would be transferred to New Orleans to assist Banks in his campaigns on the Red River in Louisiana. With three corps, Grant began his operations in late March, sending XI and XVII north-west of Vicksburg to begin working their way south.

59

On 16 April Union gunboats engaged the Vicksburg batteries as a preparatory attack to test reactions and strength. The Union navy retired after losing one boat.

On 17 April Union cavalry left La Grange, Tennessee, and rode for sixteen days through Central Mississippi towards Baton Rouge. It had the desired effect of drawing away Confederate troops from the Vicksburg defence perimeter to pursue them.

Porter's naval forces managed to slip past the Vicksburg batteries on the night of 22 April. More of Pemberton's Confederates were drawn away when Sherman's men attacked Confederate positions at Haynes's Bluff and Drumgould's Bluff.

By 19 April McPherson's troops had reached Hard Times, and on the same day Porter's fleet attacked the Confederate batteries at Grand Gulf.

On 30 April McClernand's and McPherson's corps crossed the Mississippi from Hard Times, and Sherman was sent to follow and join them.

Although Pemberton had around 40,000 men in the Vicksburg area, they were scattered, and when the Union invasion began at Port Gibson on 1 May, what troops he could bring to bear were defeated. Pemberton moved north and Grant moved north-east, where he was joined by Sherman on 8 May. Together they fought the Battle of Raymond on 12 May. Confederate General Johnston arrived at Jackson, fifteen miles to the north-east of Raymond on the 13th, taking command of the Confederate troops in that area. But on the following day the

Union army converged on Jackson, beat Johnston and cut him off from Pemberton. Johnston could only sit by and watch Pemberton's perimeter gradually shrink.

Grant left Sherman to destroy Jackson's rail facilities and industry, and with the rest of the army he headed west, following the Southern Mississippi Railroad as far as Bolton. Here he fought the Battle of Champion Hill, again beating the Confederates, which forced Pemberton to retreat to the Vicksburg defences. The Confederates turned at Big Black River Bridge on 17 May and managed to delay Grant long enough to retreat across the river and destroy the bridges behind them. Grant was not to be denied, however; he swiftly threw pontoon bridges across the river and was in pursuit again by the 18th.

Grant's forces were now converging on Vicksburg from the east and the north-east. Sherman moved to occupy the hills above the Yazoo River; this would ensure that the Confederates could not molest Grant's supply lines or routes by which reinforcements could arrive.

On 21 May, having invested the Vicksburg defences, Grant ordered his first assault. It failed, but Grant was probing to find a weakness. A second assault on 22 May was much more costly to Grant in terms of losses, and it seems that this failure convinced the Union commander that assaults against the defence works would not only fail but would seriously weaken his own forces. He determined to besiege Vicksburg and starve Pemberton out.

The siege continued through the rest of May and all of June, and gradually Grant's effective

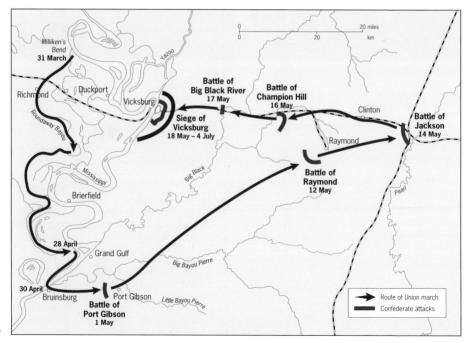

blockade was beginning to bite. Pemberton's garrison was starving and civilians in the city were reduced to living in caves. On a daily basis Grant's artillery, supported by Porter's gunboats, bombarded Vicksburg. Eventually, on 3 July,

Pemberton requested surrender terms from Grant. Characteristically there were none, apart from unconditional surrender. In fact, many of the Confederates who were paroled at Vicksburg later faced Grant at Chattanooga.

Champion Hill (Baker Creek), Mississippi, 16 May 1863
Vicksburg Campaign, 1863

Union:
Major-General Ulysses S. Grant
Army of Tennessee (3 corps)
*c.*43,000 men (15,000 engaged)
Total casualties 2,457

Confederate:
Lieutenant-General John C. Pemberton
Department of Mississippi and East Louisiana
(80 infantry regiments, 10 artillery batteries)
*c.*23,000 men
Total casualties 4,300

Following Grant's occupation of Jackson, Mississippi, the Confederates under Johnston ordered Pemberton to turn and attack Grant at Clinton. It was an audacious plan, and for some reason Pemberton chose not to carry out the order; instead he focused his attention

on the Union supply route from Grand Gulf to Raymond.

Johnston was adamant. Again on 16 May he reiterated his order to Pemberton. Pemberton turned as ordered and took up positions on the crest of Champion Hill. It did not take long before Grant closed in on Pemberton, making first contact at 07.00. Pemberton's line extended along the crest overlooking Jackson Creek. Grant threw a column along the Jackson Road, exposing the Confederates' left flank. Champion Hill itself was held by General Stephen Lee's troops, who spotted Grant's move. If Grant could not be stopped Pemberton would be cut off from Vicksburg. The Confederates moved swiftly, blocking Grant for the time being.

Grant himself arrived on the battlefield at 10.00 and immediately ordered a general assault. At 11.30 Grant's men were contesting the whole of the Confederate front line, taking the crest of the hill at

Union battle line advancing. (American Civil War Society)

61

13.00. Pemberton's men retired, but Grant's troops pushed on to capture the crossroads and close the route to Vicksburg.

Pemberton threw Bowen's Division into a counter-attack which carried the hill before running out of steam. Grant himself then counter-attacked with fresh troops which had just arrived from Clinton. The situation as far as Pemberton was concerned was getting desperate. He ordered Lloyd Tilghman's brigade to hold the Raymond Road crossing at Baker Creek whilst the rest of the army attempted to escape. Tilghman was eventually overwhelmed, and Loring's Division on the right of Pemberton's line was cut off and never made it back to Vicksburg. At least 3,000 Confederates were captured during the pursuit, which did not end until nearly midnight. By this time, Union forces had advanced as far as six miles from the battlefield. Grant had firmly placed his army between Pemberton and Johnston, and the former had to fall back on Vicksburg or run the risk of Grant taking the city.

Murfreesboro (Stone's River), Tennessee, 31 December 1862 to 3 January 1863
Stone's River Campaign, 1862–1863

Union:
Major-General William S. Rosecrans
Army of the Cumberland
c.43,400 men
(total casualties (during campaign) 13,249)

Confederate:
General Braxton Bragg
Army of Tennessee
c.37,712 men
(total casualties (during campaign) 10,266)

Following Bragg's defeat at Perryville on 8 October 1862, he fell back to Murfreesboro, Tennessee, for the winter. Here he reorganised his Army of the Mississippi into the Army of Tennessee.

Rosecrans's Union army followed Bragg out of Kentucky to Nashville, and on 26 December determined to find and beat Bragg, whom he believed to be still in the Murfreesboro area.

Rosecrans found Bragg on the night of 29 December and encamped close to the Rebel positions. Despite his ordering his men not to set fires, the Confederates were well aware that the enemy was close by. Before dawn Bragg's men attacked the right flank of the Union army. The Union troops fell back shortly after 06.00 and by 10.00 the Confederates had pushed on to the Nashville Pike. Here the Union forces held and threw back all of the successive Confederate assaults. Union reinforcements continued to arrive, further bolstering the line.

There was little fighting on New Year's Day, as Bragg was sure that Rosecrans would withdraw. However, on the morning of the 2nd Bragg was astonished to find that Rosecrans was still there and determined to fight. Bragg's cavalry had reported that Union troops were moving towards Nashville, but this proved to be incorrect as Rosecrans had positioned troops on a bluff east of the river. These troops were led by Beatty, and their presence seriously compromised the Confederate battle line.

62 *The Great Battle of Murfreesboro. (Library of Congress)*

Bragg had but two choices: either he must withdraw Polk's troops, which were now compromised, or dislodge Beatty. Despite severe opposition from his commanders, Bragg ordered Breckinridge to concentrate his division and assault Beatty. He was given ten artillery pieces and cavalry to bolster his command.

In the late afternoon Breckinridge threw a series of assaults against the Union lines east of the river. He was able, by pure numerical strength, to push them back across McFadden's Ford, but the Union troops retreated in good order and repulsed the Confederate advance with massed artillery fire. It is said that there were 58 pieces of artillery firing 100 shots a minute into the Confederate ranks. The Confederate division leading the attack lost 1,400 men.

Under this withering fire the Confederates began to give ground and started to recross the river. The Union troops then counter-attacked, recrossed the river and fell on the retreating Confederates, taking possession of the ground that they had been driven from only an hour beforehand.

Bragg later explained his reasons for withdrawing at this point in his battle report, which said: 'Common prudence and the safety of my army, upon which even the safety of our cause depended, left no doubt in my mind as to the necessity of my withdrawal from so unequal a contest.'

Bragg was finally forced to leave the battlefield on the night of 4/5 January. He retreated to Shelbyville and Tullahoma, Tennessee. Bragg had left nearly 25 per cent of his army killed or wounded on the battlefield. He had lost over 10,000 men. Union casualties were also high in particular sections of the army, with 8,788 killed or wounded and 3,489 captured.

Rosecrans did not pursue, but Bragg was forced to abandon his new positions and retire beyond the Tennessee River, ending the Stone's River Campaign on 4 July 1863. Rosecrans would now advance towards Chattanooga. The Union action had achieved its objectives of controlling the railroad between the east and the west.

The result of the battle was a significant one for the Union army, as many of their battles had been only partial victories. This time the Confederates were in full flight, as Major-General Thomas Crittenden would later recall:

'The results of the battle were not what we had hoped, and yet there was a general feeling of elation. One day, after we had gone into Murfreesboro, I accompanied General Rosecrans in a ride about our camp. We had come across some regiment or brigade that was being drilled, and they raised a shout, and as he rode along he took off his cap and said "Alright boys, alright; Bragg's a good dog, but Hold Fast's a better." This well expressed my feeling as to the kind of victory we had won.'

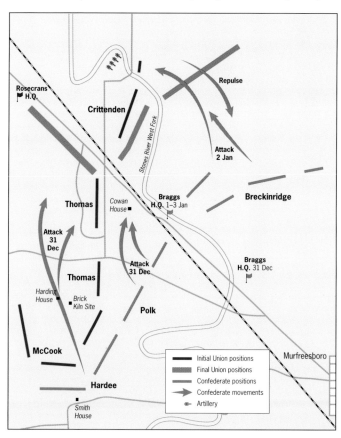

Blue Springs, Tennessee, 10 October 1863
Operations in East Tennessee, 1863

Union:
Major-General Ambrose E. Burnside
1,700 infantry, 2 batteries artillery
(total casualties 100)

Confederate:
Brigadier-General John S. Williams
c.5,000 men, plus unknown number of cavalry
(total casualties 216)

Operations in east Tennessee had begun back in early 1862. It is a mountainous area, possession of which allowed or denied co-operation between the two great Confederate armies based in Virginia and Tennessee. The Union invasion in 1862 had ended in failure on 16 May at Princeton.

On 3 September 1863, Union General Burnside occupied Knoxville with his corps. On the 7th he advanced east into Washington County, but was checked the following day at Telford's Depot. After a disastrous retreat, Union forces, under Colonel Foster, again advanced into Tennessee, meeting Confederate cavalry at Blountsville on 22 September. This time, it was the Confederates' turn to withdraw.

In late September Brigadier-General John Williams assumed command of the Confederate forces in east Tennessee and advanced on Blue Springs. Burnside was nine miles away at Bull's Gap. Williams had only 1,700 infantry and two batteries of artillery, supported by 500 newly raised men under Jackson at Greeneville. These were the only Confederate troops within a hundred miles.

Williams occupied the ridge east of Blue Springs, lighting hundreds of camp fires to give the impression of a larger force. The Union were not impressed and advanced in force against Williams on 10 October. Throughout the day, Williams's men held, but at around 17.00 hours a large column of Union troops broke through his lines. They were stopped dead by Williams's artillery.

At nightfall, facing an enemy three times his size, Williams reluctantly fell back towards Virginia. At dawn, Union cavalry which, unknown to Williams, had flanked him the day before, found him at Henderson's Hill. Williams beat off the cavalry attack and returned in good order to Leesburg.

On 4 November Williams asked to be relieved of his command. He was replaced by Colonel Giltner, who was ordered to co-ordinate an attack on Union forces under General Carter camped at Big Creek, near Rogersville, Tennessee. On the night of the 5th Giltner crossed the Holston River and advanced on Big Creek. At daylight, the following day, he fell on Carter's brigade, capturing the bulk of Union troops.

Chickamauga, Georgia, 19–20 September 1863
Chickamauga Campaign, 1863

Union:
Major-General William S. Rosecrans
Army of the Cumberland
c.57,000 men
(total casualties 16,179)

Confederate:
General Braxton Bragg
Army of Tennessee
c.71,551 men (66,326 effectives)
(total casualties 17,804)

During the summer of 1863 the Chattanooga area became the focus of both the Union and Confederate forces. It was considered to be the gateway to Georgia and the south, and for the Confederacy this meant that the area of east Tennessee and north-west Georgia was also a vital source of grain and livestock.

The terrain in the area made campaigning very difficult; there were natural obstacles. But after six months' preparation, the Union General Rosecrans launched his Tullahoma Campaign in June 1863.

Bragg's smaller Confederate army had been manoeuvred back south of the Tennessee River, which meant that Union forces could now launch a major offensive towards Atlanta and the south.

Chattanooga fell on 9 September, and the Union army moved into Georgia. They were deployed on a forty-mile front, and on the very day that Chattanooga fell, Bragg decided to launch a counter-offensive. He had been massing behind Pigeon Mountain, screened by cavalry, and during the next five days he planned to crush the over-confident Rosecrans.

On 14 September Bragg moved around the Union front to try and get himself in between Rosecrans and Chattanooga. His troops were heading for the bridges across West Chickamauga Creek on the 16th. Bragg intended to launch his assault on the 18th, but he faced contested crossings at Lee and Gordon's Mill, which postponed the attack until the 19th. By the time he had manoeuvred into position the left wing of the Union army was not where Bragg had thought it was.

Rosecrans, meanwhile, had received news that Lee was on his way to reinforce Bragg, and knew that the Confederates were planning an attack.

At dawn on the 19th both armies were on the move. Rosecrans had reinforced his left with Thomas's XIV Corps. Thomas's lead elements were operating near Reed's Bridge, where he believed he

The Battle of Chickamauga. (Library of Congress)

was following an isolated group of Confederate infantry. Little did he know that the full weight of the Confederate force was about to descend upon him.

The engagement began at 07.30, when Thomas's forward divisions encountered the Confederate army on the Reed's Bridge Road. They had run into Confederate cavalry and Walker's Confederate Corps. Both Bragg and Rosecrans, throughout the day, fed troops into the battle, with the final encounter occurring a mile north of Lee and Gordon's Mill at Viniard Farm.

While Thomas's Corps were beating back numerous attacks all along their front, Crittenden's Division, near the Chattanooga–Lafayette Road, were overrun at 14.30. Confederate troops burst through the Union centre as far as the Glenn–Kelley Road and Rosecrans's headquarters at Widow Glenn's House.

Meanwhile, at Viniard Farm, Hood's Confederates tried to push through Rosecrans's right flank, but they were pushed back as Union reinforcements arrived. As the sun set the battle petered out at around 19.00.

The armies faced one another along a six-mile front, and during the night Rosecrans contracted his front and refused his right flank. Thomas was still holding the left and believed that in the morning Bragg would strike here. Consequently Negley's

troops were sent up onto Thomas's exposed flank at around 03.00.

Meanwhile the Confederates had reorganised their army and planned to attack Thomas at dawn. As dawn broke on Sunday, the 20th, there was confusion in the Confederate command when they realised that their plans had not factored in the fact that Granger's reserve Union Corps was sitting two miles north of the Confederate right, not that far from where the major attack would take place. The Confederates finally attacked at 09.00 and managed to push through Thomas's exposed flank. Negley's Division failed to arrive, apart from one brigade, and by the time Rosecrans reacted, he was forced to throw in troops from wherever he could find them to stem the Confederate surge. Thomas managed to re-establish his line but the Confederates continued to attack. Still Thomas held. Rosecrans was determined that the road to Rossville would be held, even if he had to reinforce Thomas with his whole army.

Critically, at 11.00, just as Longstreet was about to launch his 11,000 men at the Union centre, a hole appeared in the Union battlefront, through which poured the half-mile-deep Confederate column. The Confederates flooded west towards Widow Glenn's House, the gap in the Union line growing wider as brigade after brigade were taken in the flank. Davis's men and Sheridan's Divisions of 65

McCook's Corps were routed and the Union right wing had ceased to exist.

Rosecrans's army was shattered; he had lost McCook and Crittenden, and his army was flooding back towards Chattanooga. Longstreet turned and fell on Thomas, who was desperately trying to fight a rearguard action. Thomas fell back on Snodgrass Hill, trying to hold off the Confederates whilst the rest of the army slipped away. Longstreet continued to attack, but the timely arrival of elements of Granger's Union Corps was sufficient to hold the line until 18.00, when Thomas withdrew from Snodgrass Hill. During the retreat Brigadier-General William Preston's Division failed to receive the orders to retreat, and his whole brigade was captured.

By 20.00 the battle was over and Bragg had had his victory. Longstreet, however, was furious that Forrest's cavalry had not arrived to cut off the retreating Union army.

Rosecrans fell back on Chattanooga and was besieged by Bragg. All was not lost for Rosecrans, however: Grant was on his way and Hooker arrived with 20,000 reinforcements.

By 4 November Longstreet had been withdrawn, which gave Grant the ideal opportunity to launch a counter-offensive, during which he managed to drive Bragg off in a series of battles between 23 and 25 November.

The writer Ambrose Bierce was present during Thomas's retreat towards McFarland's Gap. He said of the battle:

'Away to our left and rear some of Bragg's people set up the rebel yell. It was taken up successively and passed round to our front, along our right and in behind us again until it seemed almost to have got to the point whence it started It was the ugliest sound that any mortal ever heard – even a mortal exhausted and unnerved by two days of hard fighting, without sleep, without rest, without food, and without hope. There was, however, a space somewhere at the back of us across which that horrible yell did not prolong itself – and through that we finally retired in profound silence and dejection, unmolested.'

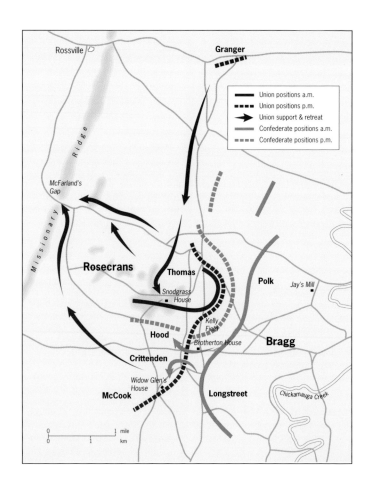

Union:
Major-General Ulysses S. Grant
Army of the Cumberland
*c.*60,000 men
(total casualties 5,815)

Confederate:
General Braxton Bragg
Army of Tennessee
*c.*46,000 men
(total casualties 6,670)

This was the third battle fought at Chattanooga, the first having taken place on 7–8 June 1862, during the Confederate Heartland Defensive. The second occurred on 16 August 1863 during the Chickamauga Campaign. Both of these battles paled into insignificance when nearly 12,500 men died as Grant faced Bragg in November 1863.

Since the Union defeat at Chickamauga, Bragg's Confederate army had laid siege to Rosecrans at Chattanooga, but on 17 October Grant took over and replaced Rosecrans with Thomas. Together they established a new supply line, and when Sherman arrived with four fresh divisions in mid-November, Grant was ready to take the offensive.

Chattanooga is on the south bank of the Tennessee River, at the northern end of a valley five or six miles wide. To the east is Missionary Ridge rising to 800 feet. On the west is Lookout Mountain, 2,200 feet

high, and just below the town of Chattanooga was the Memphis and Charleston railroad.

The Confederates were entrenched from the north end of Missionary Ridge, all along its crest, then across the Chattanooga Valley to Lookout Mountain. The mountain was fortified and Confederate pickets extended all the way down to the river.

Grant had already tried to dislodge the Confederates from Lookout Mountain, and had succeeded in securing Brown's Ferry, eight miles from Chattanooga, which would allow Union supplies and reinforcements.

Assaults by the Confederates at the end of October failed, and on 4 November Longstreet had been detached from the besieging Confederate force to attack Burnside at Knoxville.

Grant took the initiative and planned a major counter-offensive. He determined that Sherman should cross the Tennessee River at Brown's Ferry and assault Missionary Ridge. Meanwhile more troops would be sent north to support him. In order to pin the Confederates down Grant sent troops to reinforce Fort Wood, which lay between the town and Missionary Ridge.

The Confederates, occupied with this action on the afternoon of 23 November, failed to respond to Sherman's continued movement from Brown's Ferry. During the night of the 23rd artillery was ferried across the Tennessee River and work began on building a bridge to allow artillery and cavalry to cross.

Grant and his staff officers at the Battle of Chattanooga. (Library of Congress)

67

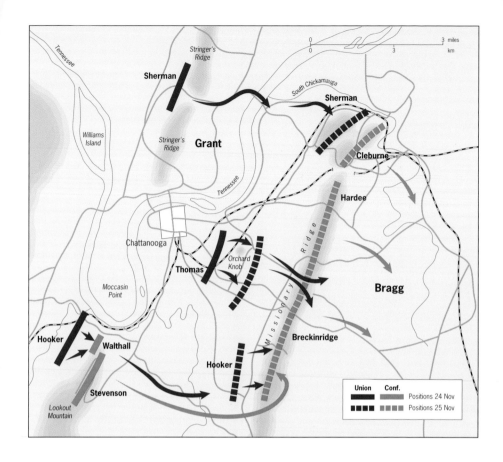

Hooker, meanwhile, had been sent west to menace the Confederates on Lookout Mountain. By the morning of the 24th Hooker had crossed the Nashville–Chattanooga Railroad and had built a bridge across Lookout Creek. By noon Hooker's men were advancing across the northern slope of the mountain towards the strong Confederate fortifications. Sherman, having bridged the South Chickamauga River, was now moving along the east of Missionary Ridge.

By 17.00 Grant was delighted to hear that Hooker had taken 2,000 prisoners and that most of Lookout Mountain was in Union hands. During the night Grant sent orders to Sherman to attack at daylight and that Hooker should support him by cutting off the Confederate retreat.

Sherman faced the most difficult proposition; the enemy were on fortified higher ground with a second fortification which could give ready support. However, by sunrise his troops were on the move. Three brigades held the north-east hill of Missionary Ridge and more troops were moving around the east and the west. The Confederates held a steep and heavily wooded ridge, and initially the Union advance carried to the extreme end of the Confederate fortifications. Sherman's troops managed to advance as far as the railroad bridge, which effectively would prevent the Confederates from bringing supplies up from Chickamauga. For two hours the Confederates con-

tested the ground, but Sherman was continually threatening Bragg's flank. Bragg continually sent up more brigades against Sherman and had deployed nearly all of his artillery to stop him. Union troops were approaching the west side of the ridge and coming under heavy fire. Here the Confederates counterattacked and pushed Sherman's men back into a wood, but a sortie forced the Confederates to retreat back to their entrenchments. Bragg sensed that he could beat Sherman, but in order to do so he had to abandon Lookout Mountain.

Hooker was moving steadily towards Missionary Ridge, but the Confederates had destroyed the bridges over Chattanooga Creek and it took him four hours to make the crossing.

In the meantime Sherman's position was becoming critical. Grant threw Wood's men, supported by Sheridan, towards Missionary Ridge. It was the last thing that Bragg had expected; they carried the Confederate positions and pursued the enemy over the crest and as far as the Chickamauga River. Here the Confederates stood in the growing darkness, but Sheridan outflanked them and more Confederates fell into Union hands, whilst the others fled.

Hooker had managed to get over the Chattanooga Creek by 15.00 and attacked the Confederate flank at Rossville. Sherman had continued to face strong opposition and was unaware of the progress that the rest of the army had made until the following morning.

The Union victory at Chattanooga had been won against all the odds. Bragg in many respects was to blame for making a number of serious errors on the day. Certainly, in sending Longstreet to Knoxville he had lost his most able field commander. Union casualties approached 6,000, but Grant had bagged 6,100 prisoners, 40 artillery pieces, 7,000 muskets and a large number of wagons. Bragg admitted to having lost 4,146 men. Bragg's army was now in full retreat, and Grant turned his attention to relieving Burnside at Knoxville. He sent Sherman with elements of the Army of the Tennessee and a corps of the Army of the Cumberland. This move forced Longstreet to aban-

don his siege; he had lost his chance to defeat Burnside's 12,000 men with his own 20,000.

The year 1863 had been disastrous for the Confederacy; they had lost at Gettysburg and at Vicksburg, and now they faced a double defeat at Chattanooga and Knoxville. Many historians have blamed Bragg for the defeat at Chattanooga and claimed that he missed an opportunity to destroy the Union army. Had he won at Chattanooga, then east Tennessee would certainly have fallen. Bragg could not have guessed at Grant's military genius and the dogged determination that characterised Sherman's approach to warfare.

Dallas (New Hope Church/Pumpkinvine Creek/Pickett's Mill), Georgia, 26 May to 1 June 1864

Atlanta Campaign, 1864

Union:
Major-General William T. Sherman
Military Division of Mississippi

(total casualties 2,400)

Confederate:
General Joseph E. Johnston
Army of Tennessee

(total casualties 3,000)

The encounters between Sherman and the Army of Tennessee towards the end of May 1864 are some of the most misunderstood of the American Civil War. There were, in fact, three pitched battles: New Hope Church, 25 May; Pickett's Mill, 27 May and Dallas, 28 May. These battles occurred when Johnston's Confederates fell back from Cassville–Kingston to the Allatoona Pass and then on to Dallas, where he entrenched. Sherman continually probed the lines throughout this rolling encounter.

It seems that Johnston's line extended from the Allatoona Pass, along the ridge of Allatoona Creek, then along Pumpkinvine Creek, with Hardy based at Dallas and Hood at New Hope Church.

The Confederates tried to hold a line at New Hope Church by entrenching in the dense thickets, but it seems that the major encounter here was between Geary's Union Division and Confederate cavalry. The Confederates had set the bridge over Pumpkinvine Creek on fire, and after the Union infantry had beaten off the enemy cavalry, the fire was put out and the bridge repaired. Hooker's infantry pushed on up the road to New Hope Church and ran into Confederates led by Hood. There was a sharp fight and the Confederates were driven back into the woods.

Two days later, a new Confederate line was encountered at Pickett's Mill, and at 18.00 Union troops rolled forward to assault. Confederate cavalry

broke up the attack, and at daylight it seemed that the Confederates were preparing to counter-attack. Sure enough, Lieutenant-General William Hardy's Corps began probing the Union defence line held by Logan, but they were repulsed with heavy losses. Despite continued reconnaissance, Sherman's Union army could not find a way around Johnston's line.

Undoubtedly the Battle of Pickett's Mill was the most significant part of this phase of the Atlanta Campaign. Sherman had been trying to get around Johnston's positions at quite a speed. He had extreme logistical problems trying to feed his vast army in enemy-held territory. When Hooker's men met resistance at New Hope Church Sherman was clearly caught off guard; he had not expected the Confederates to stand and deny him in this area. When Sherman ordered Howard towards Pickett's Mill he firmly believed that this was the left flank of the Confederate line. When Hazen's troops approached Pickett's Mill Sherman could not have realised that they were about to tackle a heavily fortified defensive position held by a Confederate commander, Cleburne. The arrival of the Confederate cavalry behind Hazen only served to confuse matters all the more. Hazen was unsupported and stranded in one of the few clear areas of the battlefield. When Wood's main attack went in at 18.00 under the command of Gibson, Cleburne routed the fresh Union infantry.

Hiram Granbury received permission to advance his Texans at around 22.00. It seems that he encountered fresh Union reinforcements who volleyed him and then withdrew. This appears to have ended the conflict at Pickett's Mill.

Eventually, on 1 June, Sherman sent Stoneman's cavalry division to the Allatoona Pass, which had the vital railroad that would allow Sherman to ship in men and supplies by train. The pass was reinforced on 3 June by Schofield's Union infantry, who had to fight a series of running skirmishes *en route*.

Sherman now occupied territory on Johnston's right and was preparing to launch a major offensive, but on 4 June Johnston fell back to a new line from Brush   69

Mountain to Lost Mountain. The significant feature of this new line was a salient called Pine Top and an outpost nearby, in front of Gilgal Church. Sherman's men continued to advance towards these new positions through the thick woodland, and dug in close to Johnston's new line. So far, Sherman had lost around 9,000 men and was reinforced by Blair's Corps, which marched from Huntsville, Alabama. By the night of 16 June, with McPherson having taken Brush Mountain and Thomas and Schofield pushing through Pine Top, the Union troops managed to capture Lost Mountain and Gilgal Church, forcing Johnston to retire again on the 16th to a new defence line which he had already prepared beyond Mud Creek.

Kennesaw Mountain, Georgia, 27 June 1864
Atlanta Campaign, 1864

Union:
Major-General William T. Sherman
*c.*16,000 men
(total casualties *c.*3,000)

Confederate:
General Joseph E. Johnston
*c.*18,000 men
(total casualties 1,000)

After Sherman left Dallas, Georgia, in steady pursuit of Johnston's Confederates, he found them entrenched on Kennesaw Mountain. He could not afford to allow the Confederates to remain here whilst he aimed to capture Atlanta because they would stand in the way of his supply lines.

This battle is particularly striking as it was waged over a ten-mile front for some $2\frac{1}{2}$ hours. Sherman's plan was simple: Schofield and Hooker would hold the Confederates under Hood in place at the southern end of the line whilst Thomas launched an assault south of Pigeon Hill. A secondary attack by McPherson would tackle the north. In this way Sherman hoped to split Johnston's army and drive through to the Western and Atlantic Railroad.

Consequently a barrage opened up on the morning of 27 June with the intention of softening up the Confederate defences. At 08.15 the Union XV Corps, under Logan, some 5,500 strong, poured forward. Meanwhile, more Union troops closed with the Confederate picket line. The main Union assault, south of the Dallas highway, got under way at 09.00 with 8,000 men committed to the attack. The seemingly unstoppable tide of bluecoats swamped the valley, crossing John Ward Creek, and further south they approached Cheatham Hill. Here and along the front they were hit by withering fire which was so intense that some of the woodland caught fire. It is said that at one stage an Arkansas colonel waved a white flag from the Confederate entrenchments and shouted, 'Come and get your men for they are burning to death'. This colonel was later given a pair of ivory-handled Colt pistols by the Union commanders for his honourable actions.

The assault was an absolute disaster; even an attempt to dig a tunnel underneath the Confederate line failed.

Union losses were crippling and were the most severe that Sherman suffered throughout his whole campaign in Georgia. The Confederates remained in place, but Johnston eventually withdrew to Atlanta on the evening of 2 July, having blunted the Union offensive.

70 *The Battle of Kennesaw Mountain. (Library of Congress)*

Peachtree Creek, Georgia, 20 July 1864
Atlanta Campaign, 1864

Union:
Major-General George H. Thomas
Army of the Cumberland
*c.*50,000 men
(total casualties 1,710)

Confederate:
General John B. Hood
Army of Tennessee
*c.*65,000 men
(total casualties 4,796)

With nearly 100,000 men in his combined armies, Sherman split his troops into three columns on the last approach to Atlanta. He knew that there was only the Chattahoochee River and the Army of Tennessee between him and the city. He sent George Thomas's Army of the Cumberland across the river to hold the Confederates in place whilst McPherson and Schofield moved east to cut the rail connection with Savannah. Sherman knew that he was facing a wily opponent in Johnston, but Jefferson Davis replaced him on 17 July with John Bell Hood, who took over the following day. The frustrations of continual Confederate retreats had enraged Davis. Hood, he hoped, would be far more aggressive and provide the victory that the South craved.

Union troops tried to cross Peachtree Creek at Howell's Mill late on 19 July, but were repulsed by the Confederates. They succeeded in crossing further east, outflanking the Confederates at Howell's Mill. Thomas organised his line about a mile wide; to the east of him were McPherson's troops, supported by Schofield.

Hood had planned to attack in force at 13.00 on the 20th, but the presence of these additional Union troops delayed him until 15.00. Hood hit three divisions of the Union army entrenched on high ground, only one of which gave way. To the Union left and right more troops came up and caught the Confederates in a devastating crossfire. Hood continued to attack, barely gaining any ground and taking huge losses.

The Confederate attacks were poorly executed as the terrain complicated any co-ordination. The area was thickly wooded, cut with creeks and choked with dense undergrowth. For five hours Hood tried to batter the Union army, but finally had to retire with grievous losses.

To hide his first failure, Hood under-reported his losses by at least 2,000 men and blamed the failure on a faulty battle plan bequeathed to him by General Johnston. His execution of the attack was, in fact, very different from what Johnston had suggested.

Atlanta, Georgia, 22 July 1864
Atlanta Campaign, 1864

Union:
Major-General William T. Sherman
Army of the Cumberland
Major-General George H. Thomas
(4 corps)
Army of the Tennessee
Major-General James B. McPherson
(3 corps)
Army of the Ohio
Major-General John Schofield
(1 corps)
(319 infantry regiments, 35 cavalry regiments and 254 guns)
(total casualties 3,641)

Confederate:
General Joseph E. Johnston
Hardee's Corps
Hood's Corps
Wheeler's Cavalry Corps
Polk's Corps
Jackson's Cavalry Division
Georgia Militia
(215 infantry regiments, plus militia, 49 cavalry regiments and 120 guns)
(total casualties 8,499)

Atlanta was the most closely fought battle of the Atlanta Campaign, following hard on the heels of Hood's defeat at Peachtree Creek two days earlier.

Hood's plan was to lure McPherson's Army of the Tennessee, which was east of Atlanta, closer to the city. He ordered Hardee's Corps on a flanking manoeuvre to hit McPherson's rear or flank. Meanwhile Hood's Cavalry Corps under Wheeler would move to cut off McPherson's supply lines.

Coincidentally, McPherson was worried about his left flank, and had placed his XVI Corps under Dodge right in the path of Hardee's route of march. Hardee's attack did not get under way until noon, instead of dawn, when they ran into Dodge's veterans. McPherson rode to the sound of the guns, right through the Union line, and was shot by Confederate sharpshooters. Sherman, in overall command of McPherson's army and Thomas's Army of the 71

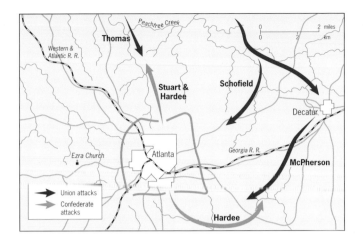

Cumberland, ordered a swift counter-attack, handing McPherson's command to 'Black Jack' Logan, with instructions to hold his ground at all costs. Led by Cleburne's division, the Confederates smashed through Dodge's lines, Maney's division headed for Bald Hill and Cheatham's straight at the Union trenches.

The Union troops around the hill, surprised and out manoeuvred, threw down their weapons but quickly realised that they outnumbered the Confederates, so they picked them up again. This time the Confederates surrendered, changed their minds and pitched into the enemy. As both sides threw in all of their available troops, the advantage swung several times. Union XV Corps commander Logan's men were in command of the hill at nightfall and Hood called off the assault.

More than 8,000 of Hood's Confederates had fallen; Sherman's armies had lost around 3,700. The attack had only been a partial success: Atlanta was still in Confederate hands (the city fell on 1 September), rail lines were open to the south and the south-west and the Union army's offensive capabilities had only been slightly blunted.

The battle of Atlanta. (Library of Congress)

Bull's Gap, Tennessee, 11–13 November 1864

Breckinridge's Expedition into East Tennessee, 1864

Union:
Brigadier-General Alvan C. Gillem
Governor's Guard Brigade, State of Tennessee
(241 casualties)

Confederate:
Major General John C. Breckinridge
Department of Western Virginia and East
Tennessee (2,400 men, casualties unknown)

In November 1864, Breckinridge began an expedition into east Tennessee, hoping that pro-Confederates in the area would rally to his cause to eject the Union troops.

Initially the thinly held area fell to Breckinridge, with the Union troops retiring onto Bull's Gap. It was essential that they should hold this position on the East Tennessee and Virginia railroad, a key supply route. Union troops occupied the position on 10 November, but Breckinridge attempted to dislodge them the following morning. The infantry assault was thrown back by 11.00, and both sides settled down to trading artillery fire with one another.

On the morning of the 12th both sides came out fighting. They clashed viciously, but neither side gained any ground. Breckinridge probed along the whole of the Union line seeking an opening or weak point, but significantly failed to dislodge the enemy.

On the 13th, Breckinridge attempted to flank the Union line, but Gillem had chosen to withdraw as he was short on ammunition and rations. His main force retired in the early hours of the 13th, leaving Colonel Miller's 13th Regiment to hold Bull's Gap until 10.30.

In the event Breckinridge managed to attack Gillem's main force near Russellville. Gillem was decisively defeated and fell back on Strawberry Plains; from there he continued his retreat to Knoxville.

Breckinridge was unable to take full advantage of his victory, as the weather was extremely poor, swelling streams and turning the roads into quagmires. But temporarily, at least, he had been able to re-establish Confederate control of east Tennessee.

By December, Union forces were back in the form of 4,000 cavalry under General Stoneman. Again Breckinridge, with a maximum of 1,500 men, intercepted Stoneman at Marion on the 18th, defeating him despite the fact that Stoneman had destroyed a lead mine and salt works in the area.

Gillem himself was back in March 1865, and this time he met with little opposition, destroying the Virginia and Tennessee railroad from Wytheville to Lynchburg. Under Stoneman's command, Gillem's troops entered Salisbury on 12 April. Gillem's men would remain on the Confederate side of the mountains until the end of the war.

Franklin, Tennessee, 30 November 1864

Franklin–Nashville Campaign, 1864

Union:
Major-General John M. Schofield
IV Corps, Army of the Cumberland (Stanley)
XXIII Corps, Army of Ohio (Cox)
*c.*22,000 infantry, 3,500 cavalry
(total casualties 2,326)

Confederate:
General John B. Hood
Army of Tennessee
3 corps
*c.*20,085 infantry, 15,500 cavalry
(total casualties 6,261)

Hood had missed a perfect opportunity to cripple the retreating Union troops at Spring Hill. Schofield's men fell back on Franklin at 01.00 and quickly erected defence works there.

Hood's Confederates were close behind, and at 14.00 hours he launched a frontal assault on the Union defence line. Despite strong opposition from two of his subordinates, Generals Cleburne and Forrest, Hood was determined to deal with Schofield once and for all.

Initially the Confederate assault was successful, pushing the two Union brigades that held the forward position aside and forcing them to retreat on the main Union positions. Along the whole of the front there was savage fighting, particularly in the Carter Farm area, which was the main linchpin of the Union breastworks. Within the yard and around the Carter house there was savage hand-to-hand fighting, during which the Carter family hid in their basement.

The impetus of the Confederate attack began to ebb and the Union line held, and when the battle finally ground to a halt Confederate casualties had reached disastrous levels. During the five-hour battle six Confederate generals were killed or mortally wounded and some of the infantry regiments had been reduced to a third of their original fighting strength.

The battle is particularly significant, if not for the outcome, for the fact that more soldiers of the Army 73

The Battle of Franklin. *(Library of Congress)*

of Tennessee died at Franklin than at Shiloh, Stone's River and the Seven Days in total. As far as the South was concerned, the Army of Tennessee died at Franklin.

Franklin is known as the Gettysburg of the West, and as one Tennessee infantryman said:

'Franklin is the blackest page in the history of the War of the Lost Cause. It was the bloodi- *est battle of modern times in any war. It was the finishing stroke to the Independence of the Southern Confederacy. I was there, I saw it.'*

At around midnight Schofield retreated towards Nashville to join General George Thomas's army, with Hood following him despite his enormous losses.

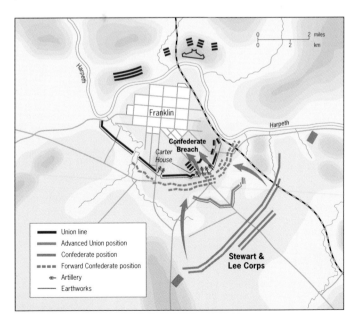

Union:
Major-General George H. Thomas
*c.*43,260 men
(total casualties *c.*2,140–2,326)

Confederate:
General John B. Hood
Army of Tennessee
*c.*37,937 men
(total casualties *c.*4,462)

In November 1864, with Major-General Sherman's troops firmly established in Georgia, General John Bell Hood, Commander of the Confederate Army of Tennessee, marched north towards Nashville to expel him from Southern soil.

Hood's men took huge casualties at Franklin on 30 November, but undaunted he continued his march towards Nashville. Unfortunately for Hood he was beaten to the town by advanced elements of Thomas's army. Hood himself did not reach

Nashville until 2 December. Overlooking the intricate fortifications that had been built by the Union engineer, Brigadier-General James St Clair Morton during 1862–3, Hood built fieldworks on the hills parallel to the Union defences.

Over a period of two weeks Thomas made elaborate preparations to crush Hood's army in the inevitable Battle of Nashville. Carefully written orders were given to each of the corps commanders. Union confidence and enthusiasm were high. The plan was that Steedman would threaten the Confederate right whilst Smith's corps and the cavalry would assault their left. Wood's men would threaten Montgomery Hill and General Schofield's troops would be held in reserve.

Union troops began to assemble at 04.00 on 15 December, and by 06.00 the men were marching out to their start positions. There was heavy fog, but by 09.00 it had cleared. Steedman's men were mainly United States Colored Troops (USCT), attacking the enemy defence works between the Nolensville and Murfreesboro Pikes; they kept Cheatham's corps busy.

The aftermath of the Battle of Nashville. (Library of Congress)

Supported by Wood's corps, the whole of the Confederate right was held to such an extent that it played no significant role in the remainder of the battle.

At around noon Wilson and Smith's troops were in position. It was decided that Beatty's Division of Wood's Corps would make an attempt on Montgomery Hill. Steadily the Union troops advanced, and amazingly they carried the Confederate works. For a moment it looked as if the attack had been repulsed, but the men pouring back were not Union infantry but captured Confederates. There was more good news on the Confederate left; Wilson's cavalry and Smith's infantry had routed the whole of the Confederate wing. The Confederates fell back from the Hillsboro' Pike to Granny White Pike, followed by Wood's and Smith's men. In places Hood had been pushed back two miles.

Rather than slip away in the night, Hood set about readying himself for the next day. At early dawn Wood's IV Corps moved forward taking up positions some 250 yards off the Confederate positions on Overton's Hill. Steedman fell in alongside him around noon. Overton's Hill was on Hood's right and his left was just west of Granny White Pike. Both had been fortified and presented formidable positions. Thomas realised that there was only one avenue of escape for Hood's army: down Franklin Pike. If he could push them off Granny White Pike, Hood's army would have to either surrender or die.

Meanwhile, on the Confederate right, Wood acceded to a proposal by Colonel Post, whose II Brigade of Beatty's Division had been instrumental in carrying Montgomery Hill the morning before, to attempt an attack on Overton's Hill. Through a storm of fire Post's men pushed forward. Post was hit and the assault failed. Steedman's USCT now attempted an assault of their own; again it was beaten back, with the loss of nearly 500 men. The attacks on Overton's Hill caused Hood to bring troops from his left.

At about the same time Union cavalry had got around the extreme left flank of the Confederates and was moving towards their rear. Thomas ordered elements of Schofield's Corps to move forward and take Shy's Hill, in front of them. They advanced with fixed bayonets and drove the Confederates out of their defence works.

On seeing this success, Beatty's Division, supported by Steedman's USCT, managed to storm Overton's Hill, and with that the whole of the Army of Tennessee was in rout. The pursuit continued for ten days and Hood's beaten men recrossed the Tennessee River, where he resigned his command.

Steedman was elated with the conduct of his men. He was a lifelong Democrat, and as his men put the Confederates to flight commented: 'I wonder what my Democratic friends over there would think of me if they knew I was fighting them with "nigger" troops?'

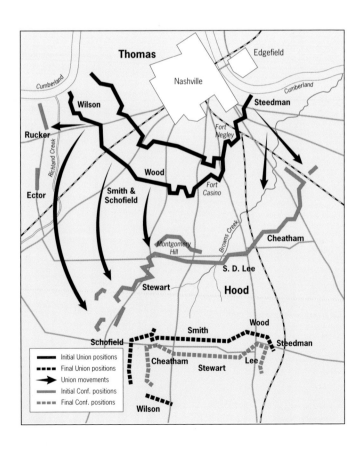

Bentonville, North Carolina, 19–21 March 1865

Sherman's March to the Sea, 1865

Union:
Major-General William T. Sherman
*c.*51,500 infantry, 4,400 cavalry, 1,700 artillerymen
(total casualties 1,646)

Confederate:
General Joseph E. Johnston
General P.G.T. Beauregard (second in command)
Army of Tennessee
*c.*15,000 infantry and artillerymen, 4,093 cavalry
(total casualties 3,092)

After burning the city of Atlanta, Georgia, Sherman marched through Confederate territory almost unmolested, shrugging off the Army of Tennessee at Franklin on 30 November 1864. He established a new base at Savannah, Georgia, in December, preparing for the long march through North Carolina with the intention of linking up with Grant.

Before Sherman's advance, the Confederates left towns and cities, such as Columbia, with no protection. On 23 February, General Joseph E. Johnston was given the task of concentrating a force which was capable of holding Sherman. If Sherman was allowed to link up with Grant, the

whole Army of Northern Virginia could be overwhelmed.

On 17 March the Confederate cavalry was in bivouac two miles from Bentonville; Johnston's main force was sixteen miles away at Smithfield. After conferring, they decided to concentrate on Bentonville and deal with the approaching Union corps as they advanced. Hampton held Bentonville using the 18th, struggling with the lead elements of Sherman's army. Johnston arrived that night, but Hardee's corps was not expected until the following morning. Sherman had been reinforcing his position in the woods and swamps either side of the Fayetteville–Goldsboro Road.

Morning found Hampton's men astride the road to Goldsboro, supported by Bragg and Stewart. Just as Hardee's men arrived, Sherman threw in an assault against Bragg (on the left of the Confederate battle line). The attack was thrown back, but had Hardee been in place, then there would have been a chance to exploit the Union withdrawal. The line had been held, but by noon the following day (20th) Sherman had arranged his whole army in front of the Confederate defence line. The Confederates threw back all of the attacks, despite being outnumbered by five to one.

On the 21st Sherman turned his attention fully on the Confederate left, only protected by cavalry pickets. Before the enemy could react to the threat

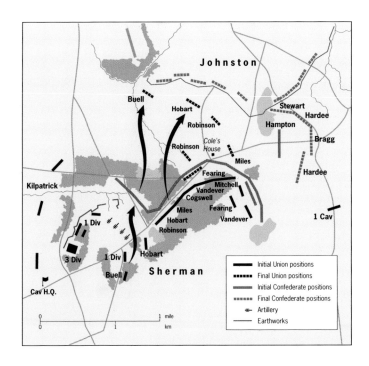

77

Sherman was throwing men across a small stream over the bridge sited conveniently to exploit the flank. The Confederates had little with which to counter the attack – barely 250 Georgian infantry and around eighty troops of the 8th Texas Cavalry. The Union troops were caught unawares and the small Confederate force threw the enemy back in confusion. Tragically Hardee's son Willie, who at the age of 16 had joined the 8th only two hours before, fell in the charge led by his own father.

Prudently, that night, Johnston pulled back his forces across Mill Creek. In the morning Sherman again tried to carry the bridge, now held by elements of Wheeler's cavalry from Hampton's cavalry corps. As the Union troops were further along the Confederate left, up to 3,000 Confederates managed to hold off Sherman's attacks. Again the lines were unbroken, but Johnston now fell back on Smithfield.

Proportionately, his losses were heavier than Sherman's.

After the battle Johnston wrote to General Lee, in part apologising for his failure to blunt Sherman's advances: 'Sherman's course cannot be altered by the small force I have. I can do no more than annoy him.'

Johnston's objective of crippling Sherman had failed; the Confederates had held their own during the sharp fight. Ultimately, Sherman would be able to seize Goldsboro and the vital railroad. The end for the Confederate States of America was close; barely three weeks remained before Lee would be forced to surrender.

The last serious attempt to hold back Sherman and defeat him in detail before his army could unite was well founded, but Sherman, having crossed hundreds of miles of enemy-lined territory, was in no mood to be denied.

Trans-Mississippi Theatre

Wilson's Creek (Oak Hills), Missouri, 10 August 1861
The Missouri Campaign, 1861

Union:
Brigadier-General Nathaniel Lyon (killed)
Major Samuel D. Sturgis
c.5,400 men
(total casualties c.1,235–1,317)

Confederate:
Brigadier-General Benjamin McCulloch
c.10,175 men
(total casualties c.1,095–1,230)

The Confederates were desperate to destroy Union forces in Missouri, and persuaded the state to join the Confederacy. Under McCulloch the Confederates moved north and camped at Wilson's Creek, ten miles from Springfield. He was to face Lyon's Union army, outnumbered more than two to one.

It was, however, Lyon who decided to attack his larger enemy, relying on the surprise element with a dawn attack. He made an overnight march to Wilson's Creek, and as luck would have it, the terrain, coupled with driving rain, meant that the Confederates were unaware of his approach. They did not discover him until shortly after dawn.

Lyon first chose to capture Bloody Hill in a manoeuvre which began at 05.30. Lyon had sent

Sigel with 1,200 men to approach the Confederate flank and rear. As Lyon's men assaulted the Confederates on the hill, Sigel's artillery opened fire. For some time there was a savage struggle for the summit of Bloody Hill, with the battle lines drawn no more than fifty yards apart. Lyon had expected Sigel to sweep up the southern slope of Bloody Hill, but McCulloch had checked him near Sharp's House.

As was common in many of the early battles, neither side was wearing standard uniform colours. When McCulloch's men approached Sigel he believed them to be some of Lyon's men, dressed in grey. McCulloch's men were equally confused, but after the initial misunderstanding the Confederates charged and Sigel's men, after a sharp fight, fled, leaving five artillery pieces.

The Confederates were now able to turn their whole attention on Lyon, even turning Sigel's guns on him. Lyon held on for five hours before the superior Confederate numbers began to tell. His artillery, deployed to the rear, was breaking up the Confederate attacks. At the crucial point Lyon was wounded, but he dragged himself onto a horse and ordered a counter-attack. He was shot in the chest, and now, with their commanding officer dead, the Union troops fell back towards Springfield.

The Battle of Wilson's Creek. The death of General Lyon. (Library of Congress)

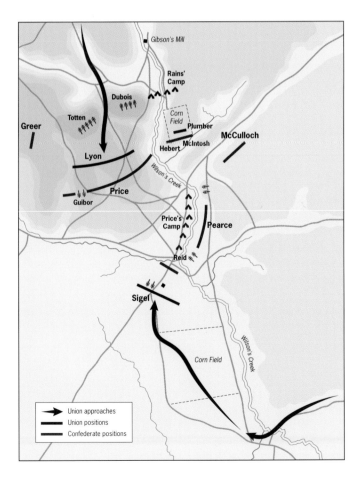

Lexington (Battle of the Hemp Bales), Missouri, 13–20 September 1861

Operations to control Missouri, 1861

Union:
Colonel James A. Mulligan
c.3,500 men
(total casualties 1,774)

Confederate:
Major-General Sterling Price
Missouri State Guard
c.12,000 men
(total casualties 100)

Following the Union defeat at the Battle of Wilson's Creek on 10 August, the Confederates launched an offensive into the Missouri River Valley. Under Sterling Price the Confederates aimed to capture the pro-Southern town of Lexington.

Under Mulligan a Union garrison entrenched itself around the grounds of the Masonic College at the north end of Lexington. Price's men marched into Lexington and pushed back the Union troops on the 13th. He then subjected them to a growing bombardment whilst he waited for his ammunition wagons and reinforcements to arrive.

On the 18th, after a nine-hour bombardment, Price launched an assault. It was heavily opposed by Union artillery but it succeeded in carrying the outer works. On the 19th, still under heavy artillery fire, the Union troops held on whilst Price consolidated his ring around their defences. In the early morning of the 20th Price launched his final assault, advancing behind mobile emplacements made of hemp bales.

Anderson House was taken, a key position, and Mulligan, having lost the majority of his officers, asked for surrender terms at around 12.00. By 14.00 negotiations were at an end and Mulligan's men surrendered. Price captured not only the remaining garrison, but five artillery pieces, 3,000 rifles, 750 horses and $900,000.

Although the Union stronghold had fallen and, for a while, the Confederates controlled the Missouri Valley, the Union commander in Missouri, Frémont, was quick to mount an offensive against Price, and he sent in 20,000 men. The Confederates were forced to retreat into south-west Missouri, leaving Lexington and the Missouri River Valley in Union hands.

The Massachusetts Volunteers fighting through the streets of Baltimore. (Library of Congress)

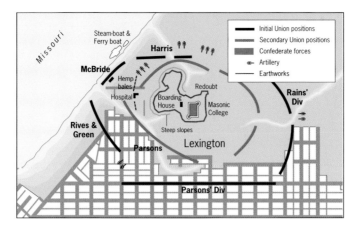

Mulligan was taken prisoner but was later exchanged and he returned to the north to resume his army career. He was killed in action at Winchester, Virginia, on 25 July 1864. Price, by September 1861, had been completely overwhelmed. He later fought further south in the war and fled to Mexico after the end of hostilities.

Pea Ridge (Elkhorn Tavern), Arkansas, 6–8 March 1862
Pea Ridge Campaign, 1862

Union:
Major-General Samuel R. Curtis
49 artillery pieces
c.10,500 men
(total casualties c.1,349–1,384)

Confederate:
Major-General Earl Van Dorn
c.16,202 men
(total casualties c.1,300–4,600)

On 29 January 1862 Van Dorn assumed command of the area which encompassed Missouri, northern Louisiana, western Arkansas and the Indian Territory. This Trans-Mississippi district was an important recruitment area for the South, and from the end of 1861 had been placed under martial law by Washington. This meant that the Union troops, under Curtis, could range far and wide, burning farms and taking whatever supplies they needed. Permanent occupation of the area, particularly Missouri, would be a great blow to the Confederacy.

Price's Confederates had abandoned Bentonville, Arkansas, shortly before 18 February when the Union troops marched in. By the 23rd Curtis had captured Fayetteville, and Price was being closely pursued by Curtis and Sigel. On 4 March Van Dorn moved towards Bentonville with a view to cutting Sigel off from the rest of the Union army. The terrain around the area slowed the Confederates down long enough for Sigel to escape as Price and Van Dorn converged.

Snow was falling heavily, but on 6 March Van Dorn and Price moved on parallel roads to close with the new Union positions on Pea Ridge near Elkhorn Tavern. The majority of the Confederates were in place by 10.00 on 7 March. They had got round the back of Curtis's men and positions, so he was forced to reverse his lines.

A significant number of the Confederates were Native American Indians, formed up into either infantry or cavalry regiments.

Price's Division approached Pea Ridge first and engaged in an artillery duel. A Confederate attack and then a Union counter-attack both failed. Confederate General McCulloch led the Confederate assault on the Union centre near Leetown. They ran into well-positioned Union infantry and were thrown back, but after re-forming the Confederates drove the enemy back.

General McCulloch was shot dead prior to four counter-attacks from the Union infantry, and Brigadier-General James McQueen McIntosh was also killed as he led five regiments of cavalry against Union artillery. At this point operations on this particular section of the battlefield ceased until around 14.00 hours.

Meanwhile the front had established itself around Elkhorn Tavern and the Tanyard area, and by nightfall the Confederates controlled areas around both the tavern and the Telegraph Road.

Shortly before daylight on the following morning, artillery opened up on both sides. Curtis had regrouped and consolidated his army, and he launched a counter-attack against the tavern area. Four assaults were held off, but the Confederate casualties were beginning to mount in number. Despite the fact that Curtis called his own men back to regroup, the continued bombardment of the Confederate centre was forcing them to retire. 81

The Battle of Pea Ridge. *(Library of Congress)*

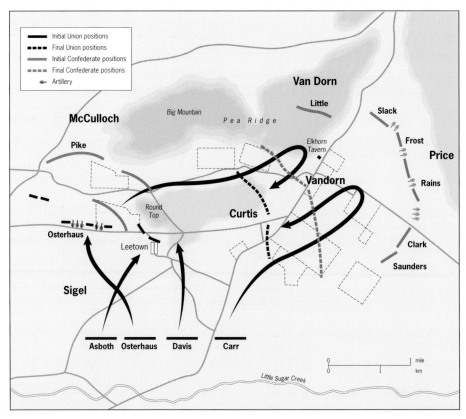

Equally, the Confederates were beginning to run out of ammunition, and Van Dorn reluctantly decided to withdraw from the field.

On 9 March Van Dorn and Curtis agreed to allow burial parties to move across the battlefield and for the exchange of wounded prisoners. It was discovered that a number of the Union dead had been scalped. Van Dorn's Adjutant-General, Colonel Maury, wrote to Curtis on this matter:

Sigel at the Battle of Pea Ridge. (Library of Congress)

'I am instructed by Major General Van Dorn, commanding this district, to express to you his thanks and gratification on account of the courtesy extended by yourself and the officers under your command to the burial party sent by him to your camp on the 9th inst. He is pained to learn, by your letter brought to him by the commanding officer of the party, that the remains of some of your soldiers have been reported to you to have been scalped, tomahawked and otherwise mutilated. He hopes that you have been misinformed. The Indians who form part of his forces have for many years been regarded as a civilised people. He will, however, most cordially unite with you in repressing the horrors of this unnatural war. That you may co-operate with him to this end more effectually, he desires me to inform you that many of our men who surrendered themselves prisoners of war were reported to him as having been murdered in cold blood by their captors, who were alleged to be Germans. The privileges which you extend to our medical officers will be reciprocated, and as soon as possible, means will be taken for an exchange of prisoners.'

Baton Rouge (Magnolia Cemetery), Louisiana, 5 August 1862
Operations against Baton Rouge, 1862

Union:
Brigadier-General Thomas Williams (killed)
Colonel Thomas W. Cahill
2nd Brigade, Department of the Gulf
c.2,500 men
(total casualties c.371–383)

Confederate:
Major-General John C. Breckinridge
c.2,600 men
(total casualties c.456–478)

In an attempt to regain Louisiana, the Confederates planned an attack on the capital, Baton Rouge, which had fallen to the Union army on 12 May 1862.

It was to be a combined arms operation, using Breckinridge's Corps and the ram CSS *Arkansas*. Breckinridge advanced from Camp Moore with 6,000 men. It was estimated that the Union garrison numbered around 3,500, with four or five gunboats in support.

Shortly after daybreak on 5 August, Breckinridge moved into the attack with Ruggles on his left and Clark on his right. Williams, the Union commander, deployed his men in a line before the town with reserves behind him. There had been no entrenchments dug and the city was open to attack from all sides except the river.

In fact, malaria, scurvy and overwork had reduced Williams's command, and at one stage earlier in the summer he had only had 800 men fit for duty. Now arranged before the advancing Confederates were, from left to right, the 4th Wisconsin, 9th Connecticut, 14th Maine, 21st Indiana and the 6th Michigan. The 7th Vermont and 30th Massachusetts formed his reserve.

The rebel ironclad ram gunboat Arkansas *on fire at the Battle of Baton Rouge. (Library of Congress)*

Ruggles's two brigades hit first, carrying everything before them, including two Union guns. The 6th Michigan counter-attacked and recaptured them, and a new line settled.

The 9th Connecticut moved on the flank and the 30th Massachusetts moved up to support, with the 4th Wisconsin advancing to help the 14th Maine, which had been stoutly holding off Clark's Confederates.

When Williams had all of his troops reordered, he signalled a general advance. No sooner had he done so than he was hit in the chest by a musket ball. He had the reputation of being a strict disciplinarian, but was noted for his courage and training.

Unperturbed by the loss of their general officer and with Colonel Cahill of the 9th Connecticut taking command, the Union troops swept forward. The Confederates offered little resistance, and by 10.00 they were retreating in disorder.

As for the *Arkansas*, her engines failed, but on the next day she closed with the Union gunboats, only to break down again. This time, her crew had to scuttle her and surrender.

Tactically, Baton Rouge was a Union victory, but strategically the situation had changed. Although the Confederates had failed to take the city, they had destroyed the bulk of the Union supplies in Baton Rouge. The action also put a stop to Union raids and patrols in the area. Of particular significance is the fact that Baton Rouge fell to the Confederate Major De Baun leading a patrol of cavalry on 21 August. It seems that the Union troops mistook De Baun's men for the vanguard of a larger Confederate force, and evacuated using the gunboats. They returned to New

Orleans and De Baun helped himself to the Union supplies.

On 19 August Breckinridge was replaced by Ruggles, and a new Confederate plan was designed with the notion of recapturing New Orleans. The plan was assigned to Major-General Richard Taylor, who was given command of troops in western Louisiana. The Union was, at the same time, concerned about the security of New Orleans. Subsequently Brigadier-General Godfrey Weitzel was placed in command of a force to dislodge Taylor from the La Fourche area.

Weitzel landed at Donaldsonville on 27 October and moved on to Thibodeaux. He encountered a 1,400-strong Confederate force under Brigadier-General Alfred Mouton at Georgia Landing, two miles from Labadieville. In this short and fierce engagement, Mouton's force was routed and pursued for four miles. Mouton retreated, burning bridges as he passed. The Confederates had lost nearly 200 men to nearly 100 of Weitzel's troops. Weitzel then camped near Thibodeaux, La Fourche was firmly in Union hands and Taylor still occupied Teche until the spring of 1863. This effectively ended operations in Louisiana until fresh plans were laid for 1863.

General Banks arrived in New Orleans on 14 December 1862 with orders to move up the Mississippi, and on 16 December 1862, General Grover was sent with twelve regiments of infantry, three batteries of guns and two troops of cavalry to recapture Baton Rouge. The next morning, the small detachment of Confederates holding the city withdrew, and Grover took Baton Rouge without having to fire a shot. It remained in Union hands until the end of the war.

Port Hudson, Louisiana, 21 May to 9 July 1863
Siege of Port Hudson, 1863

Union:
Major-General Nathaniel P. Banks
XIX Corps, Army of the Gulf
*c.*20,000 men
(total casualties *c.*5,000)

Confederate:
Major-General Franklin Gardner
Confederate Forces, Third District Department of Mississippi and Louisiana
(total casualties 7,208)

In support of Grant's Union offensive against Vicksburg, Banks was sent to tackle the Confederate stronghold of Port Hudson on the Mississippi River. It was believed to have a garrison of around 16,000 men.

By 26 May Banks had positioned about 14,000 men facing what he now believed to be the garrison of 7,000, and he ordered a general assault on the 27th. The Union troops struggled through a dense forest of magnolias and ravines, and managed to get within 200 yards of the Confederate lines. Amongst those

attacking were the African American Louisiana Native Guards, who came under a hail of fire and were beaten back with huge losses. An assault from this position proved to be impossible. The following day Union troops consolidated the siege and were still pressing Confederates into the middle of June.

On 14 June a further Union assault yielded 4,000 casualties and little more to show for the effort.

On 7 July a storming party of 1,000 volunteers had been prepared when word arrived that Vicksburg had surrendered to Grant. Initially the Confederates did not believe what had happened, but at 02.00 the following day Gardner sent a letter offering his surrender.

By the afternoon of the 8th, Union wagons entered Port Hudson with food for the Confederate garrison, and on the morning of the 9th eight regiments of Union troops marched into Port Hudson; the Confederates stacked their arms and surrendered.

It had seemed clear to Gardner that, once Vicksburg had fallen, all hope of relief had gone, and with fewer than 3,000 effectives he could not hope to hold against another determined Union assault.

85

Some 6,340 prisoners, 51 artillery pieces, 7,500 muskets and two river steamers fell into Union hands at Port Hudson. The garrison's magazines were empty.

Banks now went to Vicksburg to consult with Grant, and they agreed that the next target should be Mobile.

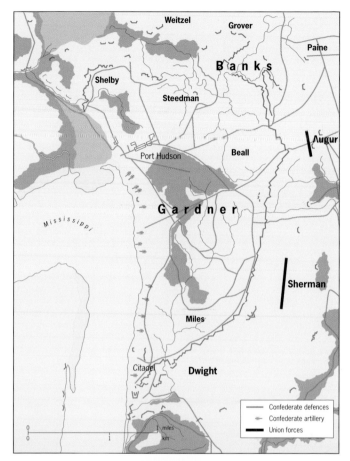

Admiral Farragut's fleet engaging the rebel batteries at Port Hudson. (Library of Congress)

Baxter Springs, Kansas, 6 October 1863
Occupation of Indian Territory North of the Arkansas River, 1863

Union:
Various detachments plus an escort
(Major-General Blunt/Lieutenant Pond)
(total casualties 103)

Confederate:
Around 400 raiders (Colonel Quantrill)
(total casualties 3)

On 17 August 1863, Colonel Blair, the Commander of the District of Kansas, ordered the construction of a fort at Baxter Springs. The camp and defence positions were established and named after Blair himself, although most referred to the fort as Baxter Springs. The outpost, commanded by Lieutenant James B. Pond, consisted of a four-foot-high log structure backed by an earth embankment, a clutch of log cabins and a cooking camp.

Colonel William C. Quantrill, a Confederate officer who led a guerrilla force in the Kansas and Lawrence area, was very active at the time. On 6 October, disguised in Union uniforms, 400 of his raiders moved on Fort Blair. After the construction of the fort, the garrison had been reduced to 25 cavalry and around 70 United States Colored Troops (USCT). Security was lax; most of the men were out foraging or eating their lunch when Quantrill's men came onto the scene.

Quantrill sent his subordinate, Poole, to deal with the fort, whilst he moved to intercept a Union detachment escorting Major-General James G. Blunt *en route* to Fort Smith, Kansas. He and his escort of 125 men, accompanied by his military band, planned to stop at Baxter Springs. The lead elements of the escort crossed the ford at Willow Creek and waited for the rest of the procession to catch up. Quantrill lay in wait until the general recommenced his march to the fort. The Confederates, in their Union uniforms, approached the column, and it was only when the general sent Captain Tough to greet them that they realised they were the enemy and not a patrol sent out by Pond.

Blunt's men were outnumbered, and many fled immediately. Quantrill pursued them for nearly two miles, killing most of them. General Blunt managed to escape, and was later removed from command for failing to take steps to protect his column. He was later reinstated, but over a hundred men had died because of his negligence.

Meanwhile, at the fort, after an initial period of confusion, the Union troops fell back behind the defences. Whilst the USCT poured carefully aimed volleys into Poole's men, Pond directed the fire with the sole 12 pdr howitzer. Poole's men were routed from the field from this unexpectedly stiff opposition.

Mansfield (Sabine Crossroads), Pleasant Grove, Louisiana, 8 April 1864
Red River Campaign, 1864

Union:
Major-General Nathaniel P. Banks
Red River Expeditionary Force
*c.*42,000 men
(total casualties 2,900)

Confederate:
Major-General Richard Taylor
District of West Louisiana
*c.*25,000 men
(total casualties 1,500)

Banks hoped to secure Southern cotton for the Northern textile mills and to make a sufficiently strong demonstration in the south to stave off any French intervention from Mexico on behalf of the Confederacy.

Banks had a considerable force at his disposal, including a 58-ship flotilla. As far as the South was concerned, it had been expecting this offensive for some time and was completely unprepared militarily to face it. Nevertheless, it was able to scrape together around 25,000 men.

The campaign opened on 10 March when the Union navy began moving up the Red River. There were a number of skirmishes and major engagements at Wilson's Farm and Ten-mile Bayou. By early April Banks had advanced 150 miles when Taylor decided that he must stand and fight or face certain disaster. He dug in around the Sabine Crossroads, four miles south of Mansfield. It was an important communications hub.

On 8 April Banks's troops began arriving in the area and managed to beat off some determined Confederate cavalry attacks. Throughout the morning of the 8th Banks probed the Confederate lines. Taylor was getting edgy, realising that as the hours passed the more Union troops he would have to face. He decided to launch an attack. Initially the Confederate offensive pushed back both of Banks's

Confederate troops in cover. (American Civil War Society)

flanks. After a running battle over three miles Banks threw in fresh troops at around 18.00, and after an hour the Confederate assault was halted. During the night Taylor again tried attacks on Banks's right, but failed.

Banks withdrew to Pleasant Hill to reorganise, with Taylor following up once again. Although this time Banks defeated Taylor, it was by no means con-clusive. Consequently Banks retreated out of Louisiana, fearing that an even greater calamity could occur if he continued to press towards his final objective of capturing Shreveport.

In many respects the battles of Mansfield and Pleasant Hill are considered to be one engagement, although the former was far more decisive in influencing Banks.

Poison Spring, Arkansas, 18 April 1864
Red River Campaign, 1864

Union:
Colonel James M. Williams
*c.*1,160 men
(total casualties 301)

Confederate:
Brigadier-General John S. Marmaduke
*c.*3,100 men
(total casualties 111)

When Steele's troops, amounting to over 13,000 men, occupied Camden on 15 April 1864, his sup-plies were virtually exhausted. His men had been on half rations for three weeks, and so he was compelled to send out a train of nearly 200 wagons, command-ed by Williams, to forage for food. The column was guarded by infantry, cavalry and two guns, whose numbers were mainly made up of the 1st Kansas Colored Volunteers.

The wagons proceeded westwards and collected corn around twenty miles west of Camden. Williams intended to collect corn from other farms on the return route. Near Poison Spring a Union relief col-umn arrived, bringing Williams's complement up to just over 1,000.

Meanwhile, Sterling Price had despatched Con-federate cavalry under Marmaduke and Brigadier-General Samuel Maxey to prevent Union foraging. Marmaduke barred the road to Camden on high ground near Poison Spring. Williams deployed his men to face them at about 09.30 on 18 April, using the wagons as a defensive line. Marmaduke attacked the front and south flanks of the wagon train, with the 1st Kansas taking the brunt of the attack. They were able to beat off Marmaduke's first charge, but when more Confederates emerged from the wooded ridge, the Union troops broke, by which time half of the Kansas men were dead or wounded. The Union line collapsed, and the Confederates showed no mercy to the black soldiers; they were hunted down and shot, even when they surrendered. Much of the butchery was blamed on the Choctaw cavalry in the Confederate ranks.

Williams retreated towards Camden as best he could, reaching safety at 11.00; he had lost four cannon, 170 wagons and 1,200 mules, and over 40 per cent of the 1st Kansas were killed or missing.

Steele's men were hit hard by the loss of the forage train, but a second supply effort arrived from Pine Bluff on 20 April. Union troops had been beaten at Mansfield and Pleasant Hill, and the Confederate Kirby Smith had just arrived in Arkansas with an additional 8,000 men.

Mobile Bay, Alabama, 5 August 1864
Operations in Mobile Bay, 1864

Union:
Rear-Admiral David G. Farragut
Union Fleet
Monitor Division – *Tecumseh, Manhattan, Winnebago, Chickasaw*
Wood Ship Division
Brooklyn, Octorara, Hartford, Metacomet, Richmond, Port Royal, Lackawanna, Seminole, Monongahela, Kennebec, Ossipee, Italsca, Oneida, Galena

Major-General E.R.S. Canby
Union Army
*c.*5,500 men (Major-General Gordon Granger)
(total casualties – Fleet: 145 killed, 170 wounded, 4 captured. Army: 7 wounded)

Confederate:
Admiral Franklin Buchanan
Confederate Fleet
Tennessee, Morgan, Gaines, Selma

Major-General Dabney H. Maury
Confederate Army
*c.*800 men
(total casualties – Fleet: 12 killed, 20 wounded, 280 captured. Army: 1 killed, 3 wounded)

The cotton-exporting city of Mobile was not a major target for Union naval forces, and even after the fall of New Orleans (April 1862) Washington was still unconvinced.

By the time that the Union Admiral Farragut was given clearance to attack the city, the defence works had been improved and Buchanan, the Confederate commander at Mobile, was threatening to break the Union blockade. Finally, Farragut had his way and the attack on Mobile was scheduled for daybreak on 5 August.

The battle opened with the *Tecumseh* firing ranging shots at Fort Morgan. Slowly the Union fleet closed, and at 07.07 the fort opened fire, which was returned by the Union battleships.

The Confederate vessels now joined in, catching the Union ships in crossfire. The *Tecumseh* was heading straight for the Confederate *Tennessee* when she was struck by a torpedo; she sank with nearly all

hands. The *Brooklyn* was taking a terrific pounding, but Farragut on board the *Hartford*, followed by the *Metacomet*, plunged through the Confederate minefield. Buchanan sent the ironclad ram *Tennessee* straight at the Union ships, with enemy steels bouncing harmlessly off her. Meanwhile, the *Hartford* shattered the *Gaines* and drove the *Morgan* away. The *Selma* closed in, but was driven off by the *Metacomet*.

In the midst of all this the *Tennessee* was desperately trying to close to ram the Union ships, but they all slipped away and dropped anchor in Navy Cove under the watchful gunners of Fort Morgan.

Incredibly the *Tennessee* had followed them; it was four miles away and closing. The *Monogahela* and the *Lackawanna* tried to ram the *Tennessee* and stop her in her tracks, but they only managed to damage themselves more than the Confederate ship. Now, the *Hartford* closed, striking the *Tennessee* head on; they sheered off one another and delivered point-blank broadsides. The *Hartford* was ripped apart, but Farragut was determined to try again.

The *Lackawanna* tried again, but only managed to get in the way of the *Hartford* and took more damage when she hit the *Tennessee.* Farragut ordered her out of the battle as the Union monsters closed in to tackle the Confederate monster. The *Chickasaw* positioned herself fifty yards astern of the *Tennessee* and bombarded her with 11in. shells. The *Tennessee's* steering chains were shot away and her smokestack collapsed. More crucially, her gun ports were jammed and Buchanan's leg was crushed when a projectile slammed against the superstructure.

The *Tennessee* could not manoeuvre, make speed or even fire back. Farragut brought up the *Manhattan* to finish her off. The *Manhattan's* 15in. guns ripped through the casements, and after three hours of fighting, the *Tennessee* surrendered at 10.00. With the loss of the *Tennessee*, the Confederate forts protecting the mouth of the bay were doomed; both fell after being stormed at great cost to the Union. Mobile's usefulness to the Confederacy was at an end; it could no longer challenge the blockade which day to day strangled the Southern states.

Farragut's victory left the Confederates with just one outlet to the sea, at Wilmington, North Carolina. Ultimately this would prove conclusive in breaking the resistance of the Confederacy.

Mobile would not fall until 12 April 1865, when General Dabney Maury's small army abandoned the city to Granger's Union troops and marched westwards to Mississippi. For nearly eight months Maury had defended the landward flank of Mobile; in effect, Mobile had become completely isolated by Sherman's march to the sea. Even then, when Mobile finally fell it cost the Union over 1,400 casualties. Grant later said; 'I had tried for more than 2 years to have an expedition sent against Mobile when its possession by us would have been of great advantage. It finally cost lives to take it when its possession was of no importance.'

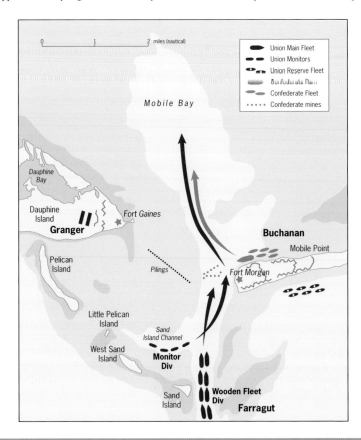

Palmito Ranch (Palmito Hill), Texas, 12–13 May 1865
Expedition from Brazos Santiago, 1865

Union:
Colonel Theodore H. Barrett
Detachments of
62nd US Colored Infantry Regiments
2nd Texas Cavalry Regiment
34th Indiana Volunteer Infantry
(total casualties 118)

Confederate:
Colonel John S. 'Rip' Ford
Detachments of
Gidding's Regiment
Anderson's Battalion of Cavalry
Sundry Confederates and Southern sympathisers

Bizarrely, there had been a gentleman's agreement between the Union and Confederate troops in the Rio Grande area since March 1865 not to fight.

Nevertheless, on 11 May Colonel Theodore H. Barrett, in command of Union forces based at Brazos Santiago, Texas, broke camp to attack Confederate outposts on the mainland. His expedition was a small one, consisting of fifty men of the 2nd Texas Cavalry Regiment, commanded by Lieutenant-Colonel David Branson, and 250 men from the 62nd US Colored Infantry Regiment.

It had been planned that the troops would cross to Point Isabel, but extremely poor weather conditions meant that they had to cross to Boca Chica. They reached the Confederate outpost at White's Ranch at

Union infantry preparing to fire. *(American Civil War Society)*

around 02.00 on 12 May. The troops deployed and surrounded the position, but it had been abandoned. Accordingly Branson decided to allow the troops to sleep along the banks of the Rio Grande, as they were exhausted after having been marching for most of the night.

At 08.30 Southern sympathisers on the Mexican side of the Rio Grande informed the Confederates of Branson's whereabouts. Branson, meanwhile, roused his men and set off to attack another Confederate outpost based at Palmito Ranch. He encountered Confederate skirmishers on his approach, but managed to close in on the position and scatter the small enemy garrison. After the fight Branson's men settled down to feed their horses and themselves and rest. But at 15.00 another Confederate force materialised. Branson decided to fall back on White's Ranch, and from here he sent a message to Barrett, who was moving up with 200 men of the 34th Indiana Volunteer Infantry, to meet him at White's Ranch, which he did at daybreak on 13 May. With these reinforcements, Branson moved forward towards Palmito Ranch, again encountering Confederate skirmishers *en route*. Once more he carried the position, but this time he destroyed all of the supplies in the depot and proceeded.

Branson pushed on a few more miles, encountering stiffer opposition, but the elusive Confederates melted away once again. Barrett encamped on a bluff at Tulosa beside the river, with the intention of spending the night there. At 16.00 Confederate cavalry under John S. 'Rip' Ford arrived, forcing Branson and Barrett to form a battle line. The Confederates had brought artillery with them and used this to good effect. Branson and Barrett were concerned that the Confederates would outflank them, and gradually they conducted an orderly retreat which succeeded in keeping Ford's men at a safe distance. The Union troops arrived back safely at Boca Chica at 20.00, and embarked back to Brazos Santiago at 04.00 the following morning.

Although this battle was little more than a series of skirmishes which did not achieve a great deal for either side, it is significant in the fact that it was the last battle of the American Civil War. In addition to this, Native Americans, African Americans and Hispanic Americans were all involved in the running fight. Another particularly significant feature was the unconfirmed reports that the Union troops came under fire from men on the Mexican side of the Rio Grande, and that Mexican regulars crossed the river into Texas during this time, but did not take part in the fighting.

It seems that as early as 1 May Confederates in the area were aware of Lee's surrender, Lincoln's death and the fact that negotiations were under way for the complete surrender of all Confederate forces. In fact several hundred Confederates deserted in the next few days.

Barrett's and Branson's final destination was Brownsville, as they heard that the Confederates were in the process of evacuating the town to move east to Corpus Christi.

At exactly the same time as the fighting was occurring around Palmito Ranch, the Confederate Governors of Arkansas, Louisiana, Missouri and Texas were authorising Kirby Smith to disband his Confederate forces and end the war. The significance of the battle at Palmito Ranch was not lost on the former Confederate President, Jefferson Davis, who wrote in his memoirs: 'Though very small in comparison to its great battles, [Palmito Ranch] deserves notice as having closed the long struggle as it opened, with a Confederate victory.'

Fort Wagner (Battery Wagner), Morris Island, South Carolina, 10–11 July 1863 and 18 July to 7 September 1863

Operations against the Defences of Charleston, 1863

Union:
Brigadier-General Quincy Gillmore
Forces engaged 18 July to 7 September,
c.5,000 men
(total casualties 10–11 July: 339,
18 July to 7 September: 1,515)

Confederate:
General P.G.T. Beauregard
Forces engaged 18 July to 7 September,
c.1,800 men
(total casualties 10–11 July: 12,
18 July to 7 September: 174)

On 10 July an amphibious Union force supported by a fleet of ironclads opened fire on Morris Island and overran two-thirds of the ground before being stopped in front of Battery Wagner. It was vital that the Confederates kept this position as it would prevent Union artillery from firing on Charleston.

The Union troops had landed on the southern tip and captured several batteries, and at dawn on 11 July Brigadier-General Strong's brigade, led by the 7th Connecticut, attacked the fort but were thrown back with heavy losses.

Gillmore reinforced his troops on Morris Island, and under the cover of dusk on 18 July a new assault, supported by heavy naval and land bombardment, was spearheaded by Colonel Shaw's Black 54th Massachusetts. They assaulted the fort with fixed bayonets and advanced into mass musketry and artillery fire. They managed to reach the parapet but after vicious hand-to-hand fighting were driven back. Shaw and hundreds of the 54th were killed or wounded.

Fort Wagner was then besieged, and it was said that a shell landed in or around the fort every thirty seconds. The Confederates held out for another 58 days before they finally abandoned Wagner in September. The Union army was then able to attack Charleston.

In the 54th's attack the 600 men led by Shaw suffered 270 casualties. Sergeant William Carney had snatched up the Union flag when the colour sergeant had been shot, and later said: 'I only did my duty; the old flag never touched the ground.' For his bravery he was the first African American to receive the Medal of Honor.

This was the fourth time that Black troops had played a key role in operations during the war, and it silenced many of the critics that had opposed Black conscription.

92   *The charge of the 54th Massachusetts Regiment and the death of Colonel Robert G. Shaw. (Library of Congress)*

Lower Seaboard Theatre and Gulf Approach

Secessionville (Grimball's Landing), James Island, South Carolina, 16 July 1863
Operations against the Defences of Charleston, 1863

Union:
Brigadier-General Alfred H. Terry
*c.*3,800 men
(total casualties unknown)

Confederate:
Brigadier-General Johnson Hagood
*c.*3,000 men
(total casualties 18)

In order to dissuade the Confederates from renewing their attacks on Fort Wagner, General Gillmore organised two separate attacks to draw off Confederate reserves. The first was an amphibious Union force that moved up the Stone's River and threatened the Charleston and Savannah Railroad Bridge. However, the second, more serious, attack was led by Brigadier-General Terry, who landed his troops on James Island on 8 July. They had arrived in order to test the Confederate defences, but on 16 July Hagood's Confederates attacked Terry's troops who had camped at Grimball's Landing.

The Confederate attack had to proceed across difficult marshy ground, and as a result was ineffective. The following day, having achieved their objective, Terry's troops withdrew from the island. Confederate General Beauregard said of 16 July: 'We attacked part of enemy's forces on James Island and drove them to the protection of their gunboats in Stone's River.'

Confederate Commander Colquitt described the action:

'I moved forward until I reached the road leading across the lower causeway. I found the enemy drawn up in battle in front of his camps. They could, I think, easily have been routed. I had proceeded, however, as far as I had instructions, and the object of the expedition having been accomplished, I returned to Secessionville.'

It appears that on the 16th, following the engagement, Hagood captured thirteen prisoners from the 54th Massachusetts. They were black soldiers, and he immediately wrote to Gillmore asking what he should do with them. He noted that two of the men had admitted to being runaway slaves; the others were free men.

This was not the first time that Union troops had tried to test the James Island defence works. On 16 June 1862 Generals Benham and Stevens, with around 6,600 men, assaulted the Confederate defences held by around 3,000. This was apparently in direct contravention to Gillmore's instructions at the time, as he had not approved a concerted assault. The net result was that Stevens's Division suffered 529 casualties out of the total Union loss of 683. The Confederates losses were estimated at around 200.

Stirling's Plantation (Fordoche Bridge), Louisiana, 29 September 1863
Taylor's Operations in West Louisiana, 1863

Union:
Major-General Napoleon J.T. Dana
2nd Division, XIII Corps
(total casualties 454)

Confederate:
Brigadier-General Tom Green
Unknown number concentrated around the Atchafalaya River
(total casualties *c.*125)

Although Union troops had been beaten at Sabine Pass earlier in September, Major-General Nathaniel P. Banks was determined to press on into Texas. After conferring with Major-General Ulysses S. Grant, it was agreed that Major-General Napoleon J.T. Dana's Division would be sent to Morganza in order to deny the Confederates the opportunity of using the Atchafalaya River. Meanwhile Banks would send his troops up the Bayou Teche and march overland into Texas.

The Union 20th Iowa Regiment under Lieutenant-Colonel J.B. Leake was sent to Stirling's Plantation to guard the road to the Atchafalaya River.

Battlefield looking south-west. The willow trees to the left of the road grow where the Norwood Sugar Mill stood. The final Confederate attack began in this vicinity and the Union troops were pushed back to the Norwood Place where heavy fighting occurred. (Dave Comeau)

Site of Stirling's plantation on north-east side of the highway. The battle took place to the right rear of the picture on the opposite side of the road from the plantation. (Dave Comeau)

The Confederate commander of the sub-district of south-western Louisiana, Brigadier-General Alfred Mouton, sensed that he had an ideal opportunity to decisively defeat the Union forces that were gathering around Fordoche Bridge. Accordingly on 19 September Brigadier-General Tom Green was ordered to move on the position. Mouton reinforced him and instructed Green to attack on the 25th. Green's men arrived at the Atchafalaya River on 28 September and by midnight on the 29th they were all across. They immediately closed on the Union picket line, with cavalry moving in first. The battle was under way by noon, and after about half an hour Green threw in the bulk of his troops and virtually surrounded the enemy. Most of the Union cavalry managed to escape, but the vast majority of the infantry and Leake were captured. Leake was later sent to Camp Ford prison camp, situated on the west of the Mississippi River.

On hearing that there had been an encounter at Stirling's Plantation, Major-General Dana despatched troops immediately. However, owing to the rainy conditions, the roads were quagmires, clogged with mud, and by the time Dana's men arrived, Green, his captives and Union stores had evacuated the area. Despite this reversal, Banks was not deterred from continuing to encroach into Texas.

Battlefield/National Park	Details
Antietam National Battlefield (near Sharpsburg)	Visitor Center Open From 08.30–17.00. Closed on Thanksgiving, Christmas and New Year's Day Tel: 301-432-5124
Appomattox Court House National Historical Park	Appomattox Court House Visitor Center/Museum Open all year Tel: 434-352-8987 ext. 26
Chickamauga & Chattanooga National Military Park (south of Fort Oglethorpe, Georgia)	Chickamauga Visitor Center 08.00–16.45. Closed on December 25 Tel: 706-866-9241 ext. 123 Lookout Mountain Battlefield Visitor Center (East Brow Road) Open from 08.00–16.45 p.m. Tel: 423-821-7786
Fort Donelson National Battlefield	Fort Donelson Visitor Center Open all year 08.00–16.30 Closed December 25 Tel: 931-232-5706
Fredericksburg & Spotsylvania National Military Park (Highway 606, 15 miles south of Fredericksburg)	Jackson Shrine Closed Wednesdays and Thursdays from the first week of April until the second week of June and from Labor Day until the last week in October. Closed Tuesday to Friday from the last week of October until the last week of March. Closed on January 1 and December 25 Tel: 804-633-6076 Spotsylvania Battlefield Exhibit Shelter (Grant Drive, 12 miles southwest of Fredericksburg) Open all year Chatham Manor (120 Chatham Lane, across Rappahannock River from Fredericksburg) Open all year 09.00–17.00 Closed January 1 and December 25 Tel: 540-654-5121

Chancellorsville Battlefield Visitor Center
(north side of Route 3, 12 miles west of
Fredericksburg)
Open all year 09.00–17.00
Closed January 1 and December 25

Tel: 540-786-2880

Fredericksburg Battlefield Visitor Center
(intersection of Lafayette Boulevard and
Sunken Road in Fredericksburg)
Open all year 09.00–17.00
Closed January 1 and December 25

Tel: 540-373-6122

Wilderness Information Centers	Wilderness Battlefield Exhibit Shelter (Route 20, 17 miles west of Fredericksburg) Open all year

Gettysburg National Military Park	Cyclorama Center (Adjacent to the National Park Service Visitor Center, 97 Taneytown Road, Gettysburg, PA 17325) Open all year 09.00–17.00 Closed on Thanksgiving Day, Christmas Day and New Year's Day Tel: 717-334-1124, ext. 422 Gettysburg National Military Park Visitor Center Open all year Closed on Thanksgiving Day, Christmas Day, and New Year's Day Tel: 717-334-1124

Harper's Ferry National Historical Park	Cavalier Heights (Adjacent to US Route 340, approximately 65 miles north-west of Washington, DC) Open all year 08.00–17.00 Closed Thanksgiving, Christmas, New Year's Day Tel: 304-535-6298

Kennesaw Mountain National Battlefield Park	Kennesaw Mountain National Battlefield Open All Year dawn–dusk Visitor center parking area 07.30–18.00 Mountain road/mountaintop 08.00–17.30 Cheatham Hill parking area 07.30–17.30 All other areas close at dusk. The mountain road is open Monday to Friday excluding major holidays. It is closed every weekend from February to Thanksgiving weekend and a shuttle bus is avail- able to ride to the top of the mountain. From Thanksgiving weekend through the end of January the mountain road is open 7 days a week from 08.00–17.30 [weather permitting] Tel: 770-427-4686

Kennesaw Mountain National Battlefield
Visitor Center
(100 yards from the intersection of Old 41 and
Stilesboro Rd)
Open all year 08.30–17.00
Closed Christmas Day

Tel: 770-427-4686

Manassas National Battlefield Park

The Henry Hill Visitor Center
Open all year 08.30–17.00

Tel: 703-361-1339

Pea Ridge National Military Park

Park Headquarters And Visitor Center
(Just off Highway 62 on the park's south side)
Open all year 08.00–17.00

Tel: 501-451-8122 ext. 227

Petersburg National Battlefield

Grant's Headquarters At City Point
(Off Cedar Lane)
Open all year 09.00–17.00
Closed Thanksgiving, Christmas Day and
New Year's Day

Tel: 804-458-9504

Five Forks Battlefield
(Right onto Route 627 – Court House Road
Travel 5.1 miles to contact station on right)
Open all year 09.00–17.00
Closed Thanksgiving, Christmas Day and
New Year's Day

Tel: 804-265-8244

Richmond National Battlefield Park

Civil War Visitor Center At Tredegar Iron Works
(Fifth and Tredegar Streets on the Richmond
Canal Walk)
Open all year 09.00–17.00
Closed New Year's Day, Thanksgiving,
Christmas Day

Tel: 804-771-2145

Cold Harbor Battlefield Visitor Center (Five miles
south-east of Mechanicsville on Route 156)
Open all year 09.00–17.00
Closed New Year's Day, Thanksgiving and
Christmas Day

Tel: 804-226-1981

Fort Harrison Visitor Center (Battlefield Park Road
off Route 5, Richmond)
Open weekends 09.00–17.00

Tel: 804-226-1981

	Glendale/Malvern Hill Battlefields Visitor Center Open all year 09.00–17.00 Closed Mondays and Tuesdays, New Year's Day, Thanksgiving and Christmas Day Tel: 804-226-1981
Shiloh National Military Park	Shiloh NMP Visitor Center Open All Year 08.00–17.00 Closed December 25 Tel: 731-689-5696
Ulysses S. Grant National Historic Site	Visitor Center (From I-270, exit to Gravois Road (Hwy 30) East and follow to left on Grant Road; site entrance is approximately one mile on right) Open all year 09.00–17.00 Closed Thanksgiving, Christmas and New Year's Day Tel: 314-842-3298
Vicksburg National Military Park	USS Cairo Museum (Milepost 7.8 along park tour road) Open all year 09.30–17.00 Tel: 601-636-2199 Visitor Center Open All Year 08.00–17.00 Tel: 601-636-0583
Wilson's Creek National Battlefield	Visitor Center Open all year 08.00–17.00 Closed Christmas Day, New Year's Day, and during periods of inclement weather Tel: 417-732-2662

Index